Simple Freezer Cookery

Caroline Rennie

COLLINS
Glasgow & London

Contents

Acknowledgments

Page 19: white and gold oval serving plate by Josiah Wedgwood and Sons Ltd., glasses from John Lewis, Oxford Street, London W1. Page 35: salt and pepper mills from John Lewis. Page 43: sauceboat from John Lewis. Page 55: picnic basket and Melaware from John Lewis, plastic containers by Frigicold. Page 63: china by Royal Albert. Page 71: clock from John Lewis. Page 79: plates by Josiah Wedgwood and Sons Ltd., Page 87: plates and vegetable dish by Josiah Wedgwood and Sons Ltd.

Designed and edited by Youé and Spooner Ltd.

Printed in Great Britain
ISBN 0 00 435171 1

Chapter 1

Your freezer

First of all, you should ask yourself why you think you want a freezer. Is it because you see it as a kind of status symbol or do you think you really need one? No one actually *needs* a freezer yet, but properly used, what a difference it makes to our lives. Changing social conditions over the last decade or so have greatly altered the housewife's life. No longer is shopping the social occasion it used to be when she went into town and spent a few hours each day choosing foodstuffs and chatting to the shopkeepers all of whom knew her by name. They were only too willing to deliver her order and, having thus exerted herself, the next stop was for a chat with her friends before setting off home for lunch and the stew she had prepared before she came out. A comparatively leisured existence beside today's hectic world of supermarkets, queues, no deliveries, dubious quality, no personal attention and an all too frequent attitude of couldn't-care-less: all this combined with the fact that many women have jobs outside the home and shopping has to be fitted into lunch hours or late evening opening times. Investing in a freezer can cut that tedious shopping to a once- or twice-monthly outing, allowing you time for that chat with your friends or at least your lunch hour to yourself in peace and quiet.

Besides the sheer convenience of having to shop less often, having a freezer means that the urban housewife can buy fresh fruit and vegetables when they are at their prime quality and lowest price and freeze them for future use. The country housewife need not be forced to give away baskets of garden peas, beans or raspberries that the family simply can't get through before the produce deteriorates – they can all be frozen. In fact, having a freezer means that you can take advantage of any bulk-buying special offers of perishable foods. Careful shopping, a beady eye and a freezer certainly pay dividends.

A freezer can also be invaluable to all those people who live alone – widows, bachelors, students, divorcees, career girls and husbands who have to stay at home and work while the rest of the family goes gallivanting off on holiday. Stocking the freezer with plenty of single servings of delicious dishes means preparation is effortless and there is no waste.

Then consider the arrival of that unexpected guest or the ones that came for tea at three o'clock and are still with you at eight o'clock, looking as if they have no intention of going. The freezer is your magic genie: there's enough for a party in it. And talking of parties, how easy a freezer makes the preparation for parties and dinners.

So there you are: all the arguments in favour of having a freezer. So choose your weapons and attack your husband in his best cheque-signing mood. Just for good measure remind him how there would be no need for that trail down to the ice cream shop on Sundays with the children – there would be masses in the freezer. Or, if that still doesn't work, just mention his favourite dish that he would be able to eat out of season! He'll soon realise how much you need a freezer.

Let us now turn to the sort of freezer that would suit you best. There are three main types – the upright model, the chest version and the refrigerator/freezer – and all have different suitabilities for different purposes. Firstly, consider the space you have available. Some people actually build on to their houses expressly to accommodate a freezer. In fact, a friend of mine did just that, then so liked the new extension to her kitchen that the freezer is now housed in the garage and the car sits out in the drive. The garage is actually an excellent place for a freezer because it is cool and dry, is accessible and yet deters constant opening of the lid which can fairly put up the inside temperature of the freezer.

Although you may have space in the kitchen for your freezer it is generally too warm a place for economical electricity running costs. You may think it would be the most convenient place but you should not really need to go to the freezer more than once or twice a day. A garage, dry outhouse or laundry room is excellent or even the cupboard under the stairs or the spare bedroom. If you put the freezer in the spare bedroom, put a cover over it and a mirror on the wall above it and, hey presto, you have a dressing table-cum-freezer! But wherever you decide to site your freezer, do make sure there's an electricity point before the delivery man arrives!

Having decided on where your new freezer is to go, the next question is size and style. If you are a single person or have a small family or live in a small flat with very little extra space, a refrigerator/freezer might well be the answer for you. This will fit well into your kitchen but do choose the coolest possible part to site it. These fridge/freezers vary in size but essentially they consist of two separate units, the lower unit being the ordinary domestic refrigerator with the other unit, the freezer, stacked on top. The freezer part may vary in size from half the capacity of the refrigerator to the equivalent capacity. But the whole unit takes up only as much floor space as your normal refrigerator. I should like to make a point here: do beware of fridges with ice boxes. These are merely conservators, not freezers and, while frozen food may be kept in the icebox in the frozen state for varying periods according to the star rating of the refrigerator, it will not actually freeze food. Manufacturers are now beginning to adopt a new system of star marking that should prevent any confusion. Four stars, one white on a blue background and three blue on a white background, as illustrated on the left, denote that the unit is a freezer.

For a bigger family in a bigger house, the choice should be between an upright or a chest model. The upright certainly takes up less floor space than the chest but it is inclined to be a little wasteful of power for, every time the door is opened, the cold air, being heavier, "falls" out of the bottom of the freezer and the hot air from the room rushes in to replace it. The electricity has then to work a bit harder to get the temperature down again. For this reason, it requires to be defrosted more often than the chest model and, unless you buy one of the self-defrosting units, this can be a tedious task. On the other hand, the design of the upright model makes it much easier to see exactly what you have in the freezer and much easier to get at it. A large upright will fit nicely into a kitchen, for instance at the end of a stretch of working space near the door, and the top of a small one may well be used as a continuation of working surface. But, as I have said, only put the freezer in the kitchen if you have nowhere else to conveniently put it.

And so we come to the chest model. These are rather ungainly and large and from all points of view are best housed somewhere other than in the kitchen. They take up a lot of floor space and the top cannot be used for storage or work space. The owner of a chest freezer has to be sure to keep a very good record of the contents because things can easily get lost in the depths. And if you are little, be careful when you are retrieving something from those depths. It's too easy to end up upside down in the freezer your legs waving in the air! However, despite the apparent problems of the chest freezer, it is much more economical to run, as the coldness does not escape when it is opened and it is, relatively speaking, less expensive to buy than the upright. Another big point in favour of this model is that big packs of meat joints and other foods can much more readily be stored in the bottom of the chest and, of course, the baskets which fit inside may be packed systematically to make selection easier.

Most freezers have locks on them which is a good idea both from the safety and the security point of view, particularly if the freezer is sited in an outhouse. After all, there is a considerable monetary investment inside that freezer. In addition, locks are a great help in keeping the children out. The temperature inside the freezer should be at −18°C or 0°F to ensure that the contents are kept in prime and safe condition, and many freezers are equipped with a warning light to show if this temperature rises. So make sure, when you go off on holiday, that you don't turn off the master electricity switch as you usually do. Imagine coming back after an expensive and super holiday in the sun to a great chest full of £90–£100 worth of soggy, totally inedible food. It is a good idea to have the freezer on an independent electrical circuit, so that for safety you can still switch off the general house electricity.

Roughly speaking, in choosing a freezer you should reckon on allowing a minimum of 2 cubic feet per member of the family and 2 cubic feet over. But most people, once they get used to making the freezer really work for its living, find that the biggest freezer there is room for and that can be afforded is the most economical proposition. It is a fact that freezer owners invariably wish they had bought a bigger freezer. So, if in doubt, buy big! It is reckoned that, for a family of four, a freezer can pay for itself in savings on food bills alone in as little as a year if properly used.

Once your freezer is installed and the engineers have checked that it is working properly it needs little care and maintenance beyond occasional defrosting, say twice or three times a year, and keeping the outside clean. If anything gets spilt inside, however, do wipe it up immediately. If you have bought a self-defrosting freezer, you are certainly going to save yourself work but if not, try to organise the defrosting when the contents are at a minimum. Take everything out, wrap each item in plenty of newspaper and put everything in a cold place. Switch off the freezer and put several basins of warm water inside. Close the door or lid and leave it for an hour or two. Then, using cloths wrung out in warm water and a little bicarbonate of soda – not soap – wipe out the inside carefully and dry it. If you need to scrape down the frost on the inside, do be sure to use only a plastic or wooden scraper. You can easily puncture the inside if you use something metal. Don't forget to wash baskets and shelves. When you have finished, close the door or lid, switch on the current and let the freezer regain its correct low temperature before you put the food back in.

If the spring breaks in the lid of the chest model, do get it fixed. It could cause a nasty accident if you don't – trapped little fingers being the least of the possible dramas!

Should the electricity fail for any reason, keep the freezer door or lid firmly shut and call the suppliers, engineer or Electricity Board for help. Most suppliers run some sort of an emergency scheme, so do ask about that when you buy your freezer. Some firms provide an all-in deal that includes freezer, food and a maintenance and emergency service. It is unlikely that you would ever lose a freezer full of food due to an electricity failure, as food will last 18–24 hours quite happily if you keep the freezer shut, and few electrical failures or strikes last that long. At any rate, many suppliers offer insurance schemes to cover food spoilage and freezer damage against just such disasters. It is worth investigating these schemes.

So now you have chosen your freezer, it is installed, working, covered for maintenance and insurance and you know how to clean it out and generally care for it. But you haven't got anything in it yet! So let's concentrate on what to stock it with and how to keep stock.

The first thing to do is to sit down and make a list of the normal things you buy each month, particularly perishables. This will give you a guide to the family eating habits and will also be a basis from which to work out what can be translated into frozen food terms. Make sure you list everything from bread and cakes to meat, fish and even canned goods because some canned foods may be translated into a frozen equivalent. I am thinking of soups particularly, where so often you use the canned or packeted varieties in preference to home-made ones because of the effort involved. (Have a look at the recipe chapter in relation to this point.) There is, of course, room on your list for one or two additional luxury items, such as the extra steak or extra cream or more specialised and expensive fruit and vegetables such as strawberries and asparagus. But don't go too mad on those things – after all, the idea is to eat better but still spend less and you won't do that if you live on best quality beef steaks!

The next thing is to get hold of a price list from a firm that specialises in supplying frozen foods for your freezer. Indeed, get hold of one or two price lists and compare range, quantity, quality and price. Don't, for goodness sake, fill your freezer with 4oz (100gm) packets of this and one portion servings of that from the freezer in your local grocers. While in certain circumstances these packs obviously have their uses, such a method of buying for your freezer would not save you money. The whole idea of a freezer is to enable you to buy in bulk.

However, stocking a freezer is an expensive business. Some firms offer a credit or budget scheme to help spread the load of payment which is a very sensible idea. After all, you are not going to eat the total contents of your freezer in one go, so why pay for it in one go? Either way, it is important to take a lot of time and care over stocking. Roughly speaking, if you are a family of four with a 14 cubic feet freezer, I would suggest you stock 3½ cubic feet of it with meat and fish, 3 cubic feet with frozen fruits in various forms and frozen vegetables, 1½ cubic feet with specialised items, such as prawn cocktails or frozen peaches, asparagus or special pies, 4 cubic feet with partly and fully prepared meals, both commercially and home-made, and 2 cubic feet with bakery items and dairy produce.

Whatever you buy, whether it is already frozen meat and pre-prepared meals or fresh fruit and vegetables to freeze yourself, do buy top quality. If you do not put top quality food into the freezer in the first place, you will not take top quality out. And if you are careful and take advantage of special offers, top quality need not cost you more.

A number of frozen food suppliers offer a composite pack of, say, £50 value and this may prove quite a good start to stocking your new freezer. It will introduce you, perhaps, to one or two commodities you have not tried before and allow you to make

up your mind about what is a good buy and what is not for your family. But do read the contents of the pack carefully. There are usually various types and there is no point in investing in one that includes 4 gallons of ice cream if the family simply will not eat ice cream.

You will also find that meat joints for the freezer are usually boned. There is no point in wasting valuable freezer space in storing bone. Some butchers will supply fresh meat at very competitive prices for you to freeze yourself but by the time it has all been individually wrapped and labelled by you and frozen in batches it may not be worth the effort. Remember that you may freeze only one tenth of the freezer's total capacity each 24 hours, and the average amount of food stored in a freezer is 30lb (approximately 15 kilo) to every cubic foot. Besides, commercially fast-frozen meat usually gives a better result than your own efforts. However, I'm not saying you ought never to freeze your own meat. There may be a time when you are given the odd joint of something special such as venison. But again, do remember, when buying frozen meat, that to spend money on the cheapest is false economy.

Freezing holds food at the state it was before it was frozen. In other words, the process causes the bacteria in the food to hibernate or, in some cases, to be killed off, but it does not either improve or destroy the food itself. However, all foods have a freezer "life" during which time the original quality, flavour and texture are retained and, while keeping foods for longer than the recommended time will do you no harm, the other essentials to enjoyment of food – texture, colour and flavour – may well be impaired. In many cases, food kept too long dries out and becomes shrunk and wizened. A slow freeze-drying process has, in effect, taken place. As a general guide, you will find that the commodities which deteriorate most quickly in their fresh state have the shortest freezer "life" and vice versa. Here is a brief table to help you:

Meat

Beef joints 12 months	Pork 10 months
Mince 8 months	Offal and sausages 4 months
Lamb 12 months	Poultry 12 months
Veal 8 months	Game 6 months

Fish

Shellfish 10 months	Oily fish 8 months
White fish 12 months	

Fruit

Citrus 6 months	Others 12 months

Vegetables

General   12 months

Dairy produce

Homogenised milk 1 month	Cream 4 months
Butter 3 months	Eggs 12 months
Hard cheese 6 months	Ice cream 3 months
Cream cheese 4 months	

Bakery

Yeast, sponge and batter mixtures 6–12 months	Pastry 3 months

Prepared meals

General 4 months	Cooked meat or poultry 1 month

Chapter 2

Clean and compact

Clean
preparation

Freezing is a method of preserving food and, as such, the same rules of cleanliness you use in other methods apply.

The first requirement, of course, when freezing food is to choose top quality foodstuffs, whether they are fresh or commercially frozen. Not only is this an important point from the flavour and texture aspect but also from the health safety angle. As I explained in the previous chapter, freezing kills off some bacteria but merely puts others to sleep. Therefore, if a commodity is reaching the point of being unsafe to eat before it is put into the freezer, by the time you take it out, thaw it and, perhaps, gently heat it through, all those germs will be ready to do their worst after their long sleep. So, the thawing out process and reheating of frozen food is also something that needs careful attention. It is very easy to roast a chicken until it appears to be cooked and nicely browned on the outside, then carve it and find that the inside, close to the carcass, is almost raw. This means that the oven heat has only just pushed its way through to the bone and, instead of being hot enough to cook the meat and kill off any bacteria which may be in the carcass, it has provided a comfortable warmth for the germs to multiply. This could, in extreme cases, lead to a degree of food poisoning.

However, remember that the frozen state is an extremely safe condition in which to hold food and while it is frozen, for however long, a food that was safe before it was frozen will never become unsafe.

A fairly common question on the subject of freezing is whether it is safe to re-freeze food. To avoid any confusion or danger I would advise you to re-freeze food only when you have changed its state. For example, you can take meat from the freezer, thaw it out, roast it, then freeze the leftovers or make it into a casserole and freeze it. Similarly, if a packet of vegetables, for instance, thaws out accidentally, cook the vegetables before re-freezing them.

Apart from the quality of the food itself, make sure that the cooking utensils and the packaging materials you are using – and your hands – are spotlessly clean. And this goes for your working surfaces too – wipe them all down with a clean cloth before you start. And while I am on the subject of general cleanliness, remember that, when you are cooling prepared food prior to putting it into the freezer, do cover it up.

So everything is in tip-top condition and scrupulously clean and you are ready to freeze some fresh foodstuffs of your own. But what do you pack them in and how do you do it?

Compact
packaging

The main essential is that whatever you use it must be moisture and vapour proof, otherwise you will get a deterioration of colour and texture of the food and what is known as freezer burn. This is the dried, leathery appearance and texture that appears on meat if it is left uncovered. Secondly, besides drying out the food, that moisture will be deposited on the walls of your freezer in the form of frost, so your freezer will require more frequent defrosting. Do not use old bread wrappers of waxed paper, bits of cellophane which were wrapped around bath salts or even a pristine piece of greaseproof paper. None of these is moisture or vapour proof. Another essential of packaging materials is that they must be strong so that they cannot be damaged by the sharp edges of other containers or careless handling. Equally, you don't want sharp meat bones to come poking through their wrapping.

At your frozen food suppliers you are sure to find a whole range of freezer packaging materials and, indeed, most big stationers now keep a good stock. The type you choose will depend on personal taste and the sort of commodities you keep in your freezer. However, as a guide, there follows a list of the basic packagings available and the food for which I consider they are best used.

Polythene bags	These are probably the most useful packaging because they are easily handled, you can put anything in them and you can see the contents at a glance. But beware of ordinary polythene bags. Some are not totally moisture and vapour proof and also the thinner ones will puncture easily or even break with the sheer weight of the food inside. They are available in various sizes, in packets or in rolls. They mould adequately round irregularly shaped foods such as chicken, and they will take buns and cakes, fruit and vegetables and even stews and liquids. If you want stews and liquids to have a regular shape when frozen, put the filled polythene bag into a suitably shaped container – square is best – and then, when it is solidly frozen, remove the container. Shaping liquids in this way makes for neatness and economy of space in the freezer. Some polythene freezer bags are, in fact, strong enough to withstand a boil-in-the-bag method of cooking but in this case you will not be able to use the bags again. Normally you can wash and re-use polythene freezer bags several times over.
Polythene film	This is sheets of clear polythene the same weight as the bags and is available in rolls. It is useful for wrapping meat and fish if you want a flat package, though its main use is as interleaving of steaks, chops, fish or sponges where you are packing several into one polythene bag or container. Film of this sort used as a covering for foil dishes or other containers is useful as it enables you to see what is in the container but don't put a container covered in this way into a hot oven. It will melt and make a mess of the food. If the dish has to be oven heated, replace the polythene with foil or remove it altogether.
Foil	Freezer foil, sometimes called heavy duty foil, is thicker than ordinary kitchen foil and has been specially designed for use in the freezer. It is bought in rolls and, for economy, it is better to buy a big roll. While foil is ideal for items such as awkward shaped joints or poultry because it will mould so closely round the irregular shape and so exclude all the air, it punctures rather more easily than strong polythene bags. It is, therefore, advisable to protect any sharp bones with a little piece of absorbent kitchen paper before you wrap the commodity. Also, it is a good idea to put the wrapped item in an outer wrap of a colour-coded polythene bag. I will explain this coding later.
Foil dishes	These are extremely useful. I save all the little foil dishes that come with commercially frozen food and re-use them for single servings, meals-on-a-plate, pies, puddings and all sorts of other things. I have a whole range of shapes and sizes. The beauty of foil dishes is that you can freeze food in them, reheat or cook it in the oven, then serve it still in the dishes. They are excellent time and effort savers. Like anything foil, however, do not use these dishes for acidic foods, such as rhubarb, lemons and so on, as the food will discolour and the foil may even erode.
Plastic boxes	These come in all shapes and sizes and are very useful and easily obtainable. They are extremely easy to use, are of a rigid, regular shape which means space saving and tidiness in the freezer and they are hygienic and clean. All sorts of foods are entirely safe in these containers, they seal well and wash easily for use over and over again. They are, however, expensive in relation to the other packaging items and this is where your personal choice comes in. I like to keep sauces, whipped cream whirls, meringues and decorated gâteaux in them because I feel the contents are best protected from breakage in this way. Also, if I want to remove only a few cream whirls at a time, for instance, the plastic box is easily opened and resealed. I use plastic boxes for easily damaged fruits, too, such as strawberries that I have previously tray-frozen myself. Empty yogurt or fresh cream pots also come into this category and these are very useful for small amounts of things.
Waxed cartons	These are best for soups and liquids in general. They come in varying sizes from $\frac{1}{4}$ pint (125ml) to 2 pints (approximately 1 litre) and can be used several times over. However, if you are using a waxed carton for something strongly coloured, such as beetroot soup, it is a good idea to fit a polythene bag inside to prevent the waxed carton from being stained. Waxed cartons are also the ideal containers for freezing fruits in syrup.
Cling film	This is relatively new on the market and is not, as yet, used much in packaging for the freezer, largely because it is rather delicate and therefore punctures easily. I find it most useful for smallish items, such as sandwiches, because they can be packed together tightly, thus preventing the filling from falling out. They can also be wrapped individually and the package is easily sealed because the cling film sticks to itself. There is therefore no need for adhesive tape or twist ties. Cling film is also useful for wrapping individual steaks and I use it a great deal for covering salads and bread to prevent them

drying out in the atmosphere. However, I do not use cling film for covering pots in the freezer. Even at double thickness, I find that it punctures too easily and is not a sufficiently strong seal.

Covering and sealing

When you are covering your packages for the freezer use lids in the case of plastic boxes, freezer foil for plastic pots without matching lids and polythene film for foil dishes. Seal the covers with strong elastic bands, freezer tape which is a special type of adhesive tape that holds at low temperatures or with paper or plastic covered, metal twist tags. All these sealers are readily available.

Also available on the market is a domestic heat sealer of the type used extensively in food factories. Much of the fresh food sold in supermarkets is sealed in this way, but, unless you are doing a tremendous amount of your own freezing and packaging in polythene, I very much doubt the economy of investing in one.

In sealing foods for the freezer, it is important to draw out as much air as possible. This can be done in several ways. If you are using rigid containers, such as plastic boxes or waxed cartons, make sure they are well filled with food to allow room inside the container for as little air as possible. The exception to this is the packaging of stews, gravies, liquids and fruits in syrup, where $\frac{1}{2}$ inch (1·2cm) headspace must be left, as the liquids expand on freezing. If you have ever found your milk on the doorstep on a frosty morning with its foil cap sitting on top of a two-inch column of frozen milk you will understand what could happen to your food inside the freezer. If you are packing light-coloured fruits in syrup it is important to hold the fruit below the surface of the liquid otherwise the fruit will discolour. Do this by putting a piece of crumpled paper into the container between the fruit and the lid. This will ensure that the fruit remains in the liquid.

There is on the market a small hand suction pump for extracting air out of packs, but really such expense is unnecessary. The way to extract air, if you are using polythene bags is to close the neck of the bag round a straw and suck the air out, catching hold of the neck of the bag tightly just below the straw when all the air is sucked out. Then close the bag tightly, using a double back fold and a covered metal tag. An alternative way is to use a weight of water. Hold the bag of food in a basin of water and let the weight of the water round the food push any air up through the neck of the bag. Seal the bag tightly and lift it out of the water. If you are going to use the boil-in-the-bag method of reheating, do make sure that, while the air is excluded from the bag, there is space inside the bag for such little air as may still remain to expand on heating. Otherwise the bag will burst.

Labelling

The packages must be labelled carefully with special stick-on freezer labels or with tie-on labels. Be sure to mark clearly on the label the contents of the package, the quantity and the date you put it in the freezer. Use a magic marker or Chinagraph pencil to mark the label, as ink or pencil blurs in the freezer.

Tidiness

Keep your freezer tidy at all times – this is important for your own ease. So you can conveniently see which commodities need replacing and which commodities should be used fairly soon and, indeed, to remind yourself of what is in the freezer, it is a good idea to develop some sort of filing system. Some people put different commodities in different coloured large string shopping bags or polythene bags – for example, bakery in blue, beef in red, lamb in green, dairy produce in yellow – so that whatever you want is easily found. I, personally, use different coloured labels because I happen to like the clean clinical look of only white boxes, clear or white polythene bags or silver freezer foil in my freezer. Just a quirk of my own, but it illustrates the point that there is no hard and fast rule. Develop your own system. Besides coloured labelling, I also keep a stock list. Mine is stuck to the inside of the lid of the freezer but you can buy books designed to keep a freezer stock – or, buy yourself a little looseleaf book. Here's a typical layout for a stock list:

Commodity	Type	Date in	No. in	No. out	Use by
BEEF	Raw mince	10/11/75	6×1 lb	lll	10/7/76
	Shepherd's pie	17/11/75	3×4 portions	ll	17/3/76

Fill it in in pencil so that details may be rubbed out when you run out of, or replenish, a commodity.

Chapter 3

Into the freezer

Home freezing

While there is an enormous range of commercially packed and frozen foods on the market which are convenient and, if bought in bulk, most economical, there are still times when you will want to freeze your own fresh foodstuffs. Perhaps you have a big garden and invariably all the vegetables seem to be ready at once, making it impossible for the family to cope with them all. The same goes for fruit, especially soft fruits which have a comparatively short season. Now, with the aid of your freezer, you can have soft fruits all year round.

Vegetables

On the whole vegetables freeze well, although they must be blanched first otherwise, on thawing, they will discolour due to enzyme reaction. It is important too that the vegetables are blanched for the correct length of time. To blanch, you need a large saucepan of lightly salted boiling water. Using a wire mesh basket which fits the pan, plunge 1lb ($\frac{1}{2}$ kilo) cleaned and prepared vegetables at a time into the water. Bring the water quickly back to boiling point and hold the vegetables there for the required length of time. Then immediately plunge the basket of vegetables into another large pan of ice-cold water and hold them there for the same length of time as they were in the boiling water. This cools them quickly and thoroughly. Drain the vegetables well on kitchen paper, pack them into containers or polythene bags and freeze.

It goes without saying that all vegetables should be in prime condition and here, for your guidance, is a chart showing which vegetables freeze well, when they are in season in Britain, how to prepare them and for how long they must be blanched before packing and freezing.

Asparagus: May–July; blanch separately for 2–4 minutes.

Broad beans: June–August; shell; 3 minutes.

Broccoli: March–May; trim evenly; 3–4 minutes.

Brussels sprouts: September–April; trim; 3 minutes.

Carrots: March–May; trim; 5 minutes.

Cauliflower: not available in April; cut into florets; 3 minutes.

Green peppers: most of the year; do not blanch – freeze raw.

Mushrooms: all year round; very fresh; do not wash or blanch.

Peas: July–August; shell; 1 minute.

Runner beans: July–September; whole if not too big; 3 minutes.

Spinach: April–November; remove coarse ribs; 2 minutes.

Sweetcorn: July–August; trim; 4–6 minutes.

Chips are a rather special case and well worth preparing in bulk. Instead of blanching the chips in boiling water, blanch them in fat for about 4 minutes. In other words, give them their first frying, then drain and cool them quickly, pack them in suitable amounts and freeze.

Do not freeze vegetables such as cabbage which is available all the year round and takes little preparation time, or root vegetables which store well. Onion rings may be frozen (blanch the rings for 1 minute) but whole onions have too high a water content to freeze successfully. The same applies to marrows and cucumbers. Salad vegetables on the whole do not freeze well and celery loses its crispness but is fine if you want to use it after freezing for a stew or as a cooked vegetable. Tomatoes take on a most peculiar flavour if frozen with the skin on but are most successful in purée form. Boiled white potatoes become mealy flavoured though new ones, almost completely cooked, freeze well.

Fruit This is frozen in a variety of ways. In the tray method the cleaned fruit is laid out on a plastic tray and put into the freezer. When it is frozen it is packed in plastic boxes. This is an excellent way of freezing soft, dark fruits that you may want to use whole later. For a dry sugar pack the fruit is lightly turned in 4oz (100gm) sugar to each 1lb (½ kilo) fruit and then packed into boxes, leaving a little headspace. Alternatively, fruit may be packed in syrup, in which case a sugar and water syrup using 1lb (½ kilo) sugar to 1 pint (approximately ½ litre) water is first made and allowed to get quite cold. Then the fruit is packed into a container, using double the weight of fruit to syrup and leaving a little headspace. Make sure the fruit is held beneath the surface of the syrup during freezing to prevent its discolouring. For your guidance, there follows a list of fruits that freeze well, roughly when they are in season in Britain, how to prepare them and which freezing method to use.

Apples: Bramleys; all year round; best frozen in purée form and packed leaving headspace or peeled, cored, sliced and blanched for 2–3 minutes, then drained, cooled and packed closely with or without sugar.

Blackberries: July–October; any of the three methods.

Cherries: June–August; remove stones; pack in syrup.

Currants: Red: July–August; any of the three methods. **Black**: July–August; any of the three methods.

Damsons: August–October; as for plums.

Gooseberries: June–July; pack in syrup.

Greengages: September; as for plums.

Loganberries: June–August; any of the three methods.

Peaches: June–August; remove stones and skin; pack in syrup.

Plums: July–September; any of the three methods (remove stones for sugar pack and in syrup).

Raspberries: June–September; any of the three methods.

Strawberries: May–September; any of the three methods.

Do not freeze fruits such as bananas, melons and pears. Bananas turn black on thawing and, although they could be used in sandwiches, they don't look very appetising. Melons are frozen commercially as melon balls but, as with pears, they are not successfully frozen at home. Due to the high water content, the texture is destroyed on thawing and they are mushy and flavourless.

Meat This, of course, freezes excellently but is best done commercially. It is frozen more quickly than a domestic freezer can do it and thereby retains more flavour. Besides, do remember that your freezer will only freeze 10 per cent of its total capacity each 24 hours – and meat takes up an awful lot of room!

Fish This also freezes well and a wide range can be bought already frozen. However, there are times when it is handy to freeze your own. It ought to be frozen within 24 hours of its being caught. Trim and gut the fish and in the case of salmon or trout, pack the inside with foil to retain a good shape. Either wrap the fish closely in polythene sheeting, seal and freeze or use the glazing method, whereby you give whole fish extra protection. Put the unwrapped fish on a piece of polythene in the freezer until very cold, then take it out and rotate it in ice-cold water. A coating of clear ice is built up on the fish. Wrap it and store in the freezer. This is an excellent way of keeping fish moist, for the ice seals it extremely well.

Poultry Freeze poultry whole or in joints, whichever is more convenient. Game must be properly hung before it is frozen, for it will not mature any more during or after freezing.

Dairy produce

Only homogenised milk freezes satisfactorily and it is quite a good idea to keep a waxed carton or two in the freezer for emergencies. Store for about one month. Cream freezes well commercially and is useful to have in the freezer, but only a high fat-content cream will freeze really satisfactorily at home. Hard cheese in a piece tends to crumble after freezing, so it is best stored grated but cream cheese freezes well and Brie and Camembert can be kept at their correct state of ripeness if frozen for short periods.

Do not freeze eggs in their shells. They will burst. However, you can freeze egg mixture. Crack the eggs into a bowl, break up the mixture with a fork and add a little salt or sugar. Store in small quantities. Alternatively, separate the yolks from the whites and freeze them that way. The whites are excellent for meringues. Again mix either sugar or salt into the yolks and label them accordingly. Hard-boiled eggs become very leathery on freezing but you could get away with a little finely chopped hard-boiled egg as a constituent of, say, a meat loaf. Do not keep butter too long in the freezer as it will alter in flavour but over a short period it can be a useful way of keeping butter bought in bulk. Baked foods and pastry freeze most successfully. Simply follow your usual recipe, leave the item to cool, then pack in a polythene bag, label and freeze. **Do not freeze** mayonnaise, as it curdles.

Cook 'n' freeze

Besides being a storage cupboard for frozen raw foods, your freezer ought also to be used for a certain quantity of prepared foods. By preparing foods at leisure when you have peace and quiet – and the energy – you certainly save a great deal of trouble and time later on when the house may be full and you may be busy with other chores. In Chapter 6 you will find all sorts of recipes to try both for and from the freezer, and as a general rule, most prepared dishes freeze very well. The way you pack your prepared dishes is up to you, but do bear in mind the manner in which you are going to serve the food. This will affect the type of pack you use, the quantity in each pack and the method of freezing. I have given an indication in each recipe as to the method of packing but as I say, it is ultimately your decision. Basically, I put pies and bakery in polythene bags, gâteaux, sauces and easily damaged things in plastic boxes, meals on foil plates, stews in bags or in foil dishes and soups and some sauces in waxed cartons.

A point worth mentioning here, perhaps, is that, when I cook a meal for the family, I very often dish one helping of everything on to a foil plate and freeze it. Then I have a meal-on-a-plate ready for a quick late meal at any time.

Prepared foods have a relatively short freezer life and there are a number of points I would like to bring to your notice in this section. Firstly, do make sure that all foods you put into the freezer are thoroughly cold beforehand, otherwise you could raise the temperature of the freezer to an unsafe level. Sauces freeze very well in small quantities but you may find they thicken a little by freezing, so either make them a little thinner than usual before you freeze them or add a little more stock or milk during the reheating process. If you find the sauce tends to separate on reheating even though you are stirring it well, try, in future, using cornflour as your thickening agent. Although it is unusual for flavours to be transferred at freezing temperatures, do not put very delicately flavoured foods near strongly flavoured curries. And, to be absolutely sure, wrap strongly flavoured foods extra well. Remember, too, that seasonings become stronger during freezing, so play them down. They can be corrected later. Some spices alter in flavour during freezing and all intensify, so go easy. Do not use nutmeg – it tastes nasty, and bear in mind that most spices take on a rather more peppery or gingery flavour. Vanilla or other types of flavourings also alter and develop an unpleasant flavour, so always use the more expensive proper essences for flavouring.

Liquids

I have talked about liquids in relation to syrups, soups, sauces and stews and told you always to leave headspace. The same applies to freezing drinks if you are going to use cartons for packaging. However, the best way to freeze drinks is in ice cube trays and then pack them in cube form in polythene bags. This way you can easily take out the quantity you require. It is quite a good idea, too, to keep a large bag of plain ice cubes in the freezer, for you know how quickly you run out of ice from the refrigerator at a party or on a hot day. Spray a little soda water into the bag of ice cubes to prevent them sticking together. *Never* put bottles of fizzy drinks into the freezer. They will explode and it could be extremely dangerous. This goes for beer too.

For a speedy meal, give the family chops topped with fried onions and served with peas and sweetcorn, all cooked straight from the freezer.

Prepare 'n' freeze

The freezer is an excellent place to keep prepared ingredients for cooking. For example, freeze whole oranges or lemons – the peel is very easily grated from the frozen state. Or, indeed, if you are having fresh orange juice for breakfast, grate the peel first, then pack it in small quantities in polythene bags or empty yogurt pots and freeze it. It is then ready for immediate use in cakes or sauces. Another good idea is to make a whole load of breadcrumbs at one go when you have the grinder on or when you have bread going stale. Pack the crumbs in 2oz (50gm) or 4oz (100gm) quantities and freeze ready for instant use anytime. The same goes for grated cheese – very useful for tops of savoury dishes, salads, soups or sauces. Then there's pastry. Make that up in bulk, divide it into suitably sized blocks and freeze them ready for use. Sometimes I even roll out and shape a few pie crusts ready to fit on top of meat or fruit to make a pie at a moment's notice. Thick or thin pancake batters, basic sauces, fruit and vegetable purée – all take a little extra time to prepare initially, so why not do them once in a while in a large quantity and freeze them in smaller quantities for future use? If you whip and slightly sweeten cream, pipe it out in whirls on to a piece of polythene sheeting in a shallow plastic box and freeze them, you have instant decorative tops for hot or cold sweets or for cakes. Fresh herbs require only to be cleaned and then popped into polythene bags and frozen. In the frozen state they crumble extremely easily so you don't have to bother chopping them. That's what I like – a minimum of effort!

Chapter 4

Out of the freezer

The question of whether or not to thaw frozen food before cooking it gives rise to all sorts of arguments among freezer owners. Some people prefer to thaw almost everything, some use food straight from the freezer, others experiment. On the whole, I prefer to thaw most things other than vegetables, unbaked pies and ready cooked meals. I think I obtain better results that way and it certainly means that I know exactly what I'm doing as regards cooking times. There is no fear of my Sunday joint being still frozen in the middle when I come to carve it. However, in most cases it is a question of both personal preference and time at your disposal.

Vegetables As there is not much density to vegetables, they are best cooked from the frozen state. Just pop them into lightly salted, boiling water and cook them for the normal length of time less the number of minutes that they were blanched. Drain them as usual and toss in butter if you like. In the case of chips, let them thaw out slightly before popping them into smoking hot, deep fat to fry and become crisp and brown. The reason for thawing them slightly is because fat cooks the outside rather quickly and the inside might not be heated through by the time the outside is done.

If you want to eat frozen fruit raw, then thaw the fruit for 8–10 hours in the unopened container in the refrigerator. If you are going to use strawberries and raspberries for decoration, it is best to spread them out on absorbent kitchen paper to thaw. This way, the juice that runs out of the fruit is soaked up and leaves the berries very dry. I grant you, it is rather wasteful of juice and a little flavour but it does result in firmer fruit. If you are using frozen fruit for cooking, then cook it slowly from the frozen state.

Meat

There are two schools of thought on the subject of thawing meat. I like to thaw meat in the refrigerator for as much as 48 hours before I cook it – though 3 hours per 1lb (½ kilo) and 4 hours per 1lb (½ kilo) for larger joints is sufficient. That way I find it is most tender and tasty. I put any juices that flow from the meat in thawing into the roasting tin, pour over the steak under the grill or add to the gravy. I waste nothing! If you do decide to cook meat from its frozen state, it is best to fry steaks and chops slowly rather than grill them, because they are inclined to lack fat in grilling, cook too quickly and toughen. And remember that they take longer to cook from frozen. Joints of meat take a great deal longer than normal to cook if you cook them from frozen but some people maintain that, properly cooked, the meat is much tastier and more tender. Put the joint into a roasting bag and roast it in a moderate oven, 350 deg F or gas 4 (180 deg C) for 50 minutes to the lb (½ kilo) for beef and veal and 60 minutes to the lb (½ kilo) for lamb and pork. Stewing meat from frozen requires almost no extra time as it is a very slow cooking process.

Poultry

This ought always to be thawed before cooking and will take about 24 hours in the refrigerator for a 3lb (1½ kilo) bird. Larger birds, such as turkeys, require 4 hours per lb (½ kilo). Small joints, such as chicken drumsticks, may be cooked from frozen if you do it slowly and make sure they are properly cooked through.

Fish

Small coated or uncoated fish may be fried fairly slowly from the frozen state but, as with meat, if you want to grill fish, thaw it in the fridge first. Large fish ought to be thawed out in the refrigerator for best results. A salmon, for example, will take 24 hours.

Soups, sauces and stews

If they are to be heated on top of the cooker they present no problem. Just allow them to thaw sufficiently to enable you to turn the contents of the pack into a saucepan, then heat through slowly but thoroughly.

Prepared meals

These have been covered in full detail in the recipe section. They are best cooked from frozen, and in a hot oven take roughly 30–50 minutes depending on size, density and type of dish.

Baked foods and pastry

Bread and rolls must, of course, be thawed before you attempt to eat them but sliced bread may be toasted very successfully from the frozen state. Bread takes about 8 hours at room temperature to thaw, but sandwiches may take only 2–3 hours. Cakes take double that time and small buns and biscuits take only about 20 minutes. On the other hand, very dense things, such as cooked meat pies can take as long as 6 hours. Let these baked goods thaw at room temperature and in their freezer bags – they stay more moist that way. It is actually quite a good idea to cut cream-filled sponges before they are completely thawed out. Similarly, fill choux pastry puffs while they are still frozen. Icing on a cake may appear to get very wet in thawing but it dries out by the time the cake is ready for eating. Pastry ought only to be thawed out sufficiently to allow you to roll and shape it but if the pie crust or the pie itself has been shaped and then frozen, bake it from frozen in a hot oven, reducing the heat when the pastry is set. This gives an excellent result.

Dairy produce

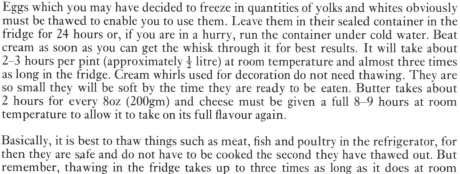

Eggs which you may have decided to freeze in quantities of yolks and whites obviously must be thawed to enable you to use them. Leave them in their sealed container in the fridge for 24 hours or, if you are in a hurry, run the container under cold water. Beat cream as soon as you can get the whisk through it for best results. It will take about 2–3 hours per pint (approximately ½ litre) at room temperature and almost three times as long in the fridge. Cream whirls used for decoration do not need thawing. They are so small they will be soft by the time they are ready to be eaten. Butter takes about 2 hours for every 8oz (200gm) and cheese must be given a full 8–9 hours at room temperature to allow it to take on its full flavour again.

Basically, it is best to thaw things such as meat, fish and poultry in the refrigerator, for then they are safe and do not have to be cooked the second they have thawed out. But remember, thawing in the fridge takes up to three times as long as it does at room temperature. Obviously, all this is relative depending on the heat of the day and how often the fridge is opened. If you want to speed up thawing, put the solidly frozen food in front of an electric blow heater turned to cold – it's amazing how quickly it works! It is not a good idea to put meat or fish or poultry into cold water, unless it is still closely wrapped, for this takes all the flavour out. But if I am going to use the meat of a chicken to make up a dish with a tasty sauce and I have forgotten to take the bird out of the freezer, I put it in a large pan of cold water, bring it very slowly to the boil and cook it that way. I then have a good pot of stock as well as a cooked chicken.

The question of whether to thaw an item in the refrigerator or at room temperature is really one of commonsense. If you would normally keep a fresh version of the food in the fridge, then thaw the frozen version in the fridge. If not, then thaw it at room temperature. In simple terms, you would not keep ordinary cakes or biscuits in the fridge so thaw them out at room temperature, but you might keep a cream gâteau in the fridge, so here's where a choice comes in. For speed, thaw at room temperature; for safety in the fridge. You may normally keep cheese in the fridge but you would take it out several hours before serving to let it take on its full flavour, so thaw frozen cheese at room temperature.

It's all really very simple when you know how!

Chapter 5

Menu planning

It is extremely easy to drift into a monotony of luxury eating when you have a freezer full of delicious steaks, strawberries and other expensive items of food, so do be careful not to fall into this trap. It is amazing how quickly one forgets the initial huge cash outlay on food and then proceeds to choose all sorts of expensive foods from the freezer in the fond notion that they are free. The whole idea of a freezer is to eat better and spend less – not spend more!

Freezer owning means planning. In fact, you really need to adopt a whole new attitude to shopping and cooking. Instead of planning meals day by day, you ought to plan ahead in weeks. After all, you are buying in bulk, so it is only sensible to plan in bulk, otherwise you may find that all the steaks and joints have been eaten and you are left with endless stewing cuts in the freezer.

When planning menus from the freezer, consider not only variety but also the food value of meals. Variety is essential to encourage people to eat and enjoy food but food value is essential too for good health. Perhaps it is worthwhile here to dwell a little on nutrition. Long before people consciously thought about nutrition, nature had a way of looking after things herself. If the colour balance of a meal was correct, then one could be pretty sure that the meal included the correct variety of nutriments for good health. This is, of course, a very simple way of deciding whether a meal is well-balanced or not but it is still an excellent guide today. Think of a meal of roast lamb, creamed potatoes, Brussels sprouts and a little redcurrant jelly – a very ordinary meal but consider the colours. There's juicy, reddish-brown meat, creamy white potatoes, fresh, green vegetables and a touch of red sauce. And in that meal there is protein, fat, carbohydrate, minerals and vitamins. Now imagine chips, sausages and fried bread – all brown and not at all colourful. There is virtually no protein, negligibly few minerals and vitamins but a lot of carbohydrate. It is neither colour balanced nor nutritionally balanced and it certainly doesn't look very appetising. So when you're planning your menus from the freezer, have an eye to colour.

Basically speaking, there are three groups of nutriments in food. They are the body-building group, the energy-giving group and the protective group and all are essential for good health.

Protein does most of the body-building work and generally keeps the body in good condition. It is contained in meat, fish – particularly oily fish – eggs, cheese and milk, and pulses such as peas and beans. Energy and warmth are derived from carbohydrates and fat which are contained in foods such as flour, potatoes, sugar, cereals and,

Well balanced meals from a well planned freezer: vegetable soup, meat pie and a raspberry mousse for an everyday meal; prawn cocktail, roast chicken and a lemon meringue pie for a weekend treat and melon balls, lobster and chocolate gâteau for a really special occasion.

of course, animal and vegetable fats. A correct intake of this group is necessary and is burnt off in energy. It is when you take too much and sit around all day doing nothing that you gain extra inches. But remember, too, that energy can mean either physical or nervous energy. It is not a good idea to cut out carbohydrates and fats altogether, for they are needed in the body for the correct functioning of the digestive system and in some cases to change minerals and vitamins into a form acceptable by the body.

The protective group are the minerals, such as calcium, contained in cheese and milk, and iron from liver and kidney and the vitamins. Vitamin A (contained in milk and vegetables) is needed to keep the eyes, nervous system and skin in good, infection-fighting fettle. The vitamin B group is contained in pork and bacon, meat extracts and foods made with wholemeal flour or oatmeal. This vitamin works against sores on the lips and mouth, keeps muscles and nerves in trim and makes carbohydrate release its warmth and energy-giving properties to the body. Vitamin C, contained in green vegetables, potatoes and dark-coloured fruits, along with iron, keeps colds and anaemia at bay. Calcium works with vitamin D to make bones good and strong. Old and young alike need this vitamin, for an insufficient amount can give rise to rheumatism – particularly in the pelvis. In extreme cases, a deficiency can lead to rickets, a disease that is still sometimes found among youngsters living in poor districts of cities. It is largely due to the lack of sunlight and fresh air on their skins, for vitamin D comes from the sun. It also comes from fatty foods, so you begin to see how closely allied are all the nutriments in food. The last one worth mentioning here is vitamin E. That, like so many other nutriments, comes from meat, milk and eggs and is the one that keeps both internal and external skin surfaces in a well-fed, supple condition – an absolute must for good muscle tone!

When planning menus, along with colour and the need for a good balance of all the nutriments, you also need to consider the occupation of the family. Do not, for instance, give your husband, who is sitting at an office desk all day, as much carbohydrate as you give the youngsters who are burning up energy at a tremendous rate. On the other hand, they all need protein for growth and development. Consider, too, the season of the year. You need warmth-giving meals in winter and light, energy-giving meals in summer.

In the next chapter you will find lots of recipes. They are divided into sections and, within each section, the recipes combine to give balanced meals. I hope they will set you on the right foot towards planning your menus, so that you will obtain the best value, in the broadest sense of the word, from your freezer.

Chapter 6

On to the table

Quick snacks

One of the many advantages of owning a freezer is that, in however much of a rush you are, there will always be something nourishing and quick to eat. Perhaps on a Wednesday the children rush in from school and rush out again to Cubs or Brownies; perhaps the men in the family are off to a football match; and what about yourself? If you are going out you hardly have time to turn round, let alone put a proper meal on the table. All these situations call for quick but nutritious snacks.

There is, of course, a wide range of commercially prepared frozen dishes on the market, such as pizzas, pies and delicious fish dishes but I am sure you must have a few of your own favourite recipes. So, surprise the family. Make a few family favourites as and when time allows, pop them in the freezer and then just quickly heat them up. Hey presto, a super snack with no apparent time or effort spent.

In this section, you will find dishes which are quickly eaten and are relatively light – just the thing for when you are in a rush. I have designed the recipes to make eight servings and have suggested how they might best be packed. However, you probably know yourself what quantities are most useful for your family.

Crispy Sausage Rolls
(Illustrated on page 23)

This is an excellent quick snack which can be eaten in the fingers if you are in a real hurry.

Serves 8	**16 slices white bread**	**2lb (1 kilo) sausagemeat**
	2 teaspoons made mustard	**fat for frying**
	1 teaspoon mixed herbs	**parsley**

To make
Trim the crusts off the bread, spread each slice with a little mustard and sprinkle with herbs. Divide the sausagemeat into 16 pieces, then roll each piece to the length of a slice of bread. Put each piece of sausage on a piece of bread and wrap the bread round the sausage. Secure with a cocktail stick. Fry the rolls in hot, shallow fat, turning them constantly to brown evenly and cook through. Drain the rolls on kitchen paper and leave them to cool.

To freeze
When the sausage rolls are cold pack them in a plastic box with a piece of polythene between each roll. Seal, label, date and freeze.

To finish
Preheat the oven to moderate to moderately hot, 375 deg F or gas 5 (190 deg C). Take the required number of rolls out of the freezer. Place them on a greased baking tray and put them in the oven for 30 minutes to heat through thoroughly.

To serve
Serve hot, wrapped in a paper napkin and garnished with plenty of parsley.

Cheese Dreams with Bacon

A tasty quick snack that can be almost ready in the freezer.

Serves 8

16 back bacon rashers
6oz (150gm) butter
16 slices white bread
12oz (300gm) Cheddar cheese

bacon fat
8 eggs
8 tomatoes

To make

Trim the rind from the rashers and grill the bacon. Meanwhile, butter the bread and slice the cheese. Make up eight sandwiches using the bread, cheese and grilled bacon. Trim the crusts and cut the sandwiches in four.

To freeze

Pack the sandwiches into a plastic box, seal, label, date and freeze.

To finish

Take the required number of sandwiches out of the freezer. Heat some bacon fat in a frying pan and fry the sandwiches slowly to melt the cheese inside and to crisp and brown the outside. Fry one egg per person at the same time.

To serve

Serve the Cheese Dreams with a fried egg and a fresh tomato.

Spaghetti Bolognaise

It is best to freeze the Bolognaise sauce and cook the spaghetti fresh when it is required. This way, the sauce may be used with a variety of savoury dishes.

Serves 8

½ pint (250ml) frozen chicken stock
8oz (200gm) frozen minced beef
3 tablespoons olive oil
2 shallots
2 medium onions
2 garlic cloves
1lb (½ kilo) tomatoes

1 small can tomato purée
1oz (25gm) sugar
3 teaspoons oregano
1 teaspoon basil
salt
1lb (½ kilo) spaghetti
4oz (100gm) frozen grated cheese

To make

Take the chicken stock from the freezer and leave it to thaw out slightly. Turn the frozen minced beef into a saucepan and heat it very gently to thaw it out. Turn up the heat a little and brown the mince. Meanwhile, heat the olive oil in a heavy based saucepan. Peel and finely chop the shallots and onions and fry gently in the oil until tender but not brown. Add the peeled and crushed garlic cloves and the skinned and sliced tomatoes. Cook until the tomatoes are soft. Mix in the purée, sugar and herbs, then add the mince and chicken stock. Bring the sauce to the boil, cover it and allow it to simmer gently for 1 hour. Check the seasoning.

To freeze

Turn the Bolognaise sauce into a basin, cover and set it aside to cool quickly and thoroughly. Put the mixture in conveniently sized waxed cartons or yogurt cartons. Seal, label, date and freeze.

To finish

Cook the required amount of spaghetti in lightly salted, boiling water until tender. Drain. Meanwhile, turn the required amount of sauce into a saucepan and heat thoroughly.

To serve

Put a portion of hot spaghetti on individual serving plates, pour sauce over and sprinkle the top of each portion with ½oz (12gm) grated cheese.

Bought frozen pizzas, crispy sausage rolls (page 21), a glass of milk and some fruit make a light but nutritious meal-in-a-hurry.

Savoury Macaroni

Macaroni makes an excellent snack meal but it does take a little time to prepare. Cut that time to a fraction by using the freezer.

Serves 8

12oz (300gm) macaroni
salt
oil
8oz (200gm) back bacon rashers
1lb (½ kilo) tomatoes

4oz (100gm) butter
2 teaspoons thyme
2oz (50gm) frozen toasted
   breadcrumbs

To make

Wash the macaroni and put it into lightly salted, boiling water. Simmer until the macaroni is tender. Drain and rinse the macaroni in cold water to cool it quickly. Place it in a bowl and toss in a little oil to stop it sticking together. Grill the bacon rashers and chop them. Skin and slice the tomatoes and fry in the butter until the tomatoes are reduced to a purée. Mix in the thyme and chopped bacon. Pour the tomato mixture over the macaroni and mix it all well together.

To freeze

Cover the macaroni and set aside to cool quickly and thoroughly. Put the mixture into eight single-size foil dishes and cover with kitchen foil. Put the dishes carefully into a large polythene bag, seal, label, date and freeze.

To finish

Preheat the oven to moderate to moderately hot, 375 deg F or gas 5 (190 deg C). Take the required number of dishes of macaroni out of the freezer and remove the polythene bag. Place the dishes on a baking sheet and put into the oven for about 30 minutes. After 15 minutes' cooking time, remove the foil cover from each dish and sprinkle toasted breadcrumbs over the surface to crisp and brown the top.

To serve

Serve either in the foil dishes on a plate, or carefully spooned out on to hot plates.

Chicken Risotto

This is a good way of using up leftovers and also having a tasty quick snack "on tap".

Serves 8

2 medium onions
3oz (75gm) butter
8oz (200gm) rice
1 pint (approximately ½ litre)
   chicken stock
salt

pepper
1–2 teaspoons mixed herbs
8–12oz (200–300gm) cooked chicken
   meat
frozen parsley

To make

Chop the onions finely. Melt the butter in a strong saucepan, add the onions and fry until lightly brown. Add the rice and fry until it is brown. Pour in the stock and add salt, pepper and herbs to taste. Bring to the boil and boil rapidly for 10 minutes. Chop the chicken meat and add to the pan. Then turn the heat down and simmer slowly until the rice has absorbed all the liquid.

To freeze

Turn the risotto into a basin, cover and set aside to cool quickly and thoroughly. Divide it into conveniently sized portions and put in polythene bags. Seal, label, date and freeze.

To finish

Take the required quantity of risotto from the freezer and turn it into a saucepan with ⅛ pint (63ml) water to each single portion of risotto. Break the risotto down with a wooden spoon over a gentle heat. Make sure the risotto is thoroughly heated.

To serve

Serve the Chicken Risotto piping hot with a little frozen parsley crumbled over the top.

Kidneys on Toast

This is a really delicious quick snack.

Serves 8

8oz (200gm) button mushrooms
3oz (75gm) butter
16 lamb's kidneys
2oz (50gm) flour
salt

pepper
½ pint (250ml) red wine
8 frozen slices white bread
frozen parsley

To make

Toss the washed mushrooms in a little of the butter melted in a frying pan. Remove them from the pan and set them aside. Halve, skin and core the kidneys, then toss them in flour seasoned with salt and pepper. Heat the remaining butter in the frying pan and fry the kidneys gently for a few minutes. Add the wine and the mushrooms to the pan. Simmer gently for 30 minutes. Blend the remaining flour with a little water, and add gradually to the pan, stirring well until the sauce thickens.

To freeze

Turn the kidneys on to a dish, cover and set aside to cool quickly and thoroughly. Pack into conveniently sized plastic boxes or clean yogurt cartons, seal, label, date and freeze.

To finish

Take the required quantity of kidneys from the freezer and allow them to thaw out slightly. Turn them into a saucepan and heat gently to boiling point. Meanwhile, take the required number of frozen slices of bread from the freezer and toast them on both sides.

To serve

Serve the kidneys very hot piled on slices of trimmed toast. Crumble frozen parsley on top for garnish.

Mushroom Toasts

Serve these as a piquant snack or in smaller quantities as hot cocktail savouries.

Serves 8

4oz (100gm) butter
12oz (300gm) frozen sliced
   mushrooms
1½oz (37gm) frozen breadcrumbs
salt

cayenne pepper
8 small slices white bread
2 cans smoked herring roes
watercress

To make

Melt 1oz (25gm) of the butter in a small pan. Add the mushrooms, breadcrumbs and salt and cayenne pepper to taste. Mix well together. Melt the remaining butter in a frying pan and fry the bread slices until they are crisp and golden. Remove from the pan and spread each slice with mushroom mixture. Set aside to cool quickly and thoroughly.

To freeze

When the Mushroom Toasts are cold, put them on a tray and cover them with a piece of polythene film. Put them into the freezer. When they are frozen, pack them in plastic boxes, seal, label, date and return to the freezer.

To finish

Take the toasts from the freezer and put them under a slow grill to thaw out and heat through. Top each with smoked roes and turn up the heat to crisp and brown the tops.

To serve

Serve each garnished with watercress. Alternatively, cut them into smaller pieces for cocktail savouries.

Cauliflower Cheese

It is always useful to have a quantity of cheese sauce in the freezer.

Serves 8	4oz (100gm) butter	salt
	4oz (100gm) flour	pepper
	2 pints (approximately 1 litre) milk	2lb (1 kilo) frozen cauliflower
	8oz (200gm) frozen grated cheese	frozen crumbled cooked bacon

To make   Melt the butter in a large saucepan. Stir in the flour and cook it gently for 1–2 minutes. Remove the pan from the heat and gradually beat in the milk until you have a smooth, coating sauce. Return the pan to the heat, stir in the grated cheese and beat until smooth. Season with salt and pepper.

To freeze   Turn the sauce into a basin. Put a piece of buttered paper over the surface of the sauce to exclude the air and so prevent a skin forming. Set the sauce aside to cool quickly and thoroughly. Pack it in conveniently sized containers, seal, label, date and freeze.

To finish   Take the required quantity of sauce from the freezer and allow it to thaw out a little to enable you to get it out of the container. Meanwhile, take the required quantity of cauliflower from the freezer and cook it in lightly salted, boiling water. Turn the sauce into the top part of a double boiler or into a small basin in a pan of boiling water. Heat it thoroughly, stirring all the time to prevent it separating. Drain the cauliflower.

To serve   Serve the cauliflower with the sauce poured over it and crumbled bacon sprinkled liberally on top.

Welsh Rarebit

With your freezer you can produce this old favourite in half the time it used to take.

Serves 8	8oz (200gm) frozen grated Cheddar cheese	salt
		cayenne pepper
	4 tablespoons milk	8 frozen slices white bread
	4oz (100gm) butter	4 tomatoes
	4oz (100gm) frozen white breadcrumbs	frozen parsley

To make   Put the cheese, milk and butter into a saucepan and cook gently until the cheese is melted. Mix in the breadcrumbs and season with salt and cayenne pepper to taste.

To freeze   Cover the mixture and set it aside to cool quickly and thoroughly. Put a sheet of polythene on a large tray and divide the cheese mixture into eight piles on the polythene. Spread each pile out to a square approximately the size of a slice of bread. Cover the tray with another piece of polythene sheeting and put the tray in the freezer. When the cheese is frozen, take the tray from the freezer, cut the polythene between each piece of cheese and put the frozen pieces of cheese and polythene backing into a polythene bag. Seal, label, date and return to the freezer.

To finish   Take the required number of pieces of cheese from the freezer and remove the polythene. Take the required number of frozen slices of bread from the freezer and toast them on one side only. Put a piece of frozen cheese on the untoasted side of each slice of bread. Toast under a medium grill to heat, melt and brown the cheese.

To serve   Top each Welsh Rarebit with half a tomato sliced and a sprig of frozen parsley.

Lamb curry with noodles (page 29) accompanied with dishes of coconut and mango chutney, chopped cucumber and sliced tomatoes, and sliced banana with wedges of lime.

Late meals

I don't know about you, but when I get home late, I simply cannot be bothered cooking a proper meal. I used to end up having a marmalade sandwich and a glass of milk but it is changed days now that I have a freezer.

However, there's another aspect to late meals. Perhaps you are one of those poor, unfortunate wives who never knows what time her hard-worked husband is going to arrive home for his meal. With your freezer, your problems are over. When your husband eventually arrives home, pop a dish of something from the freezer into the oven and, by the time he has had a wash and you have both sat down and relaxed a little, his dinner will be ready. No fuss, no bother – no bad tempers!

Or perhaps you've been to the theatre? When you get home, pop whatever meal you want from the freezer into the oven and by the time you have had a drink by the fireside and done an efficient post-mortem on the play, your meal will be ready – and you won't have broken the euphoric spell or burnt the potatoes in your daze!

Chicken Liver Pâté
(*Illustrated on page 79*)

It is useful always to have a variety of pâtés in the freezer, as they can be used as starters to a meal, for savouries or cocktail snack spreads.

Serves 10–12		
1lb ($\frac{1}{2}$ kilo) chicken livers		2 bayleaves
6oz (150gm) butter		salt
2 shallots		pepper
1 teaspoon thyme		2 tablespoons brandy
1 teaspoon basil		10–12 slices white bread
1 teaspoon marjoram		lettuce and tomato for garnish

To make   Line a 1lb ($\frac{1}{2}$-kilo) loaf tin with kitchen foil. Cut the livers up roughly and melt the butter in a small saucepan. Pour a little butter into a frying pan and gently fry the livers and the chopped shallots. Add the herbs, salt and pepper. Cook gently. Remove the bayleaves, then turn the mixture into a blender and blend to a fine consistency. If you have no blender, put the liver mixture through a mincer twice or rub it through a coarse sieve. Mix in the remaining melted butter and the brandy. Spoon the mixture into the lined loaf tin.

To freeze   Cover the tin with kitchen foil, then set aside to cool quickly and thoroughly. Put it in the freezer. When frozen, remove the tin and overwrap the foil-wrapped pâté in more kitchen foil. Seal, label, date and return to the freezer. Alternatively, after preparing the pâté set it in the refrigerator until it is really cold, then remove it from the tin and carefully cut it into 10–12 portions. Wrap each portion separately in polythene and put them in a plastic box. Seal, label, date and freeze.

To finish   Take the pâté or required portions of pâté from the freezer and leave to thaw out before unwrapping. Toast a slice of bread for each person, then cut each slice of toast into fingers.

To serve   Serve the pâté with a little lettuce and tomato for garnish. Accompany with hot toast.

Lamb Curry with Noodles

(Illustrated on page 27)

This dish uses up leftovers from the Sunday roast and makes an excellent late meal.

Serves 6

2oz (50gm) desiccated coconut
1 pint (approximately ½ litre) stock
1 medium onion
2 apples
2oz (50gm) butter
1oz (25gm) curry powder
2oz (50gm) flour
1lb (½ kilo) cold, cooked lamb
1 tablespoon mango chutney
1 tablespoon lemon juice

salt
6oz (150gm) egg noodles
2 tablespoons oil
desiccated coconut
mango chutney
sliced tomato
chopped cucumber
sliced banana
lime or lemon wedges

To make

Soak the coconut in the stock. Peel and chop the onion and the apples. Melt the butter in a pan and fry the onion and apples. Stir in the curry powder and cook for 20 minutes. Blend the flour with a little water, then add it gradually to the mixture in the pan, together with the strained stock. Stir continuously until the sauce reaches boiling point, then simmer for a further 20 minutes. Cut the lamb into pieces and add it, together with the chutney and lemon juice, to the sauce. Season with salt and simmer for a further 5 minutes. Cook the noodles, drain, rinse and toss in the oil.

To freeze

Put the noodles into three greased, two-portion, foil pie dishes and pour a third of the lamb curry over each. Cover the dishes with foil and set them aside to cool quickly and thoroughly. Seal, label, date and freeze.

To finish

Preheat the oven to moderately hot, 400 deg F or gas 6 (200 deg C). Take the required number of dishes of curry out of the freezer and place them on a baking sheet. Put into the oven for 30 minutes to heat through thoroughly.

To serve

Turn the curry and noodles out on to a serving dish. Accompany it with dishes of desiccated coconut, mango chutney, sliced tomato, chopped cucumber and sliced banana with wedges of lime or lemon.

Carrot Soup

Soups are excellent for late meals – warming, nutritious and easily digestible.

Serves 6

3 pints (approximately 1½ litres)
   water
4 chicken stock cubes
1 bayleaf
1 bouquet garni

salt
2 medium onions
2lb (1 kilo) frozen carrots
½ pint (250ml) milk
frozen parsley

To make

Put the water in a large saucepan and crumble in the chicken stock cubes. Add the bayleaf, bouquet garni and salt. Peel and chop the onions, then add them, together with the carrots to the stock. Bring the soup to the boil, half cover it with a lid and simmer gently for 1 hour. Remove the bayleaf and bouquet garni. Either rub the soup through a hair sieve or put it in a blender so that the vegetables are puréed.

To freeze

Turn the soup into a basin, cover and set it aside to cool quickly and thoroughly. Pour the soup into one- or two-portion waxed cartons. Seal, label, date and freeze.

To finish

Take the required quantity of soup from the freezer, allow it to thaw out a little, then turn it into a saucepan. Heat it slowly. Stir in about 2 tablespoons milk to each portion.

To serve

Serve the soup piping hot in soup bowls sprinkled with crumbled frozen parsley.

Leek and Barley Soup

This is a delicious warming soup which is excellent at the end of a long, hard day.

Serves 6

3 frozen chicken joints
3 pints (approximately 1½ litres) water
6 medium leeks
1 stick celery

1½oz (37gm) pearl barley
bouquet garni
salt
frozen parsley

To make

Put the frozen chicken joints into a large saucepan with the water and bring slowly to the boil. Wash and slice the leeks and celery and add to the saucepan, together with the barley, bouquet garni and salt to taste. Return the soup to boiling point and half cover it with a lid. Simmer for about 1½ hours, or until the chicken is falling off the bones. Carefully remove the chicken joints from the soup and take all the meat off the bones. Chop the meat and return it to the soup. Discard the bones. Remove and discard the bouquet garni.

To freeze

Turn the soup into a basin, cover and set it aside to cool quickly and thoroughly. Remove any fat from the surface. Pour the soup into one- or two-portion waxed cartons. Seal, label, date and freeze.

To finish

Take the required quantity of soup from the freezer, allow it to thaw out a little, then turn it into a saucepan. Heat it slowly and thoroughly.

To serve

Pour the piping hot soup into soup bowls, sprinkle frozen parsley on top and serve with crusty French bread and butter.

Mince Balls in Tomato Sauce

Once prepared and frozen, this dish needs only heating up and serving.

Serves 6

2lb (1 kilo) frozen minced beef
4 medium onions
8oz (200gm) rice
salt
pepper

2 teaspoons thyme
2 cans condensed tomato soup
1¼lb (¾ kilo) frozen mixed vegetables
frozen parsley

To make

Take the mince from the freezer and allow it to thaw out completely. Preheat the oven to cool, 300 deg F or gas 2 (150 deg C). Chop the onions very finely. Mix together the mince, onions, rice, salt, pepper and thyme and form into 12 balls. Put the mince balls in a greased pie dish and pour the tomato soup over. Cover the dish with kitchen foil and bake in the oven for 1½ hours.

To freeze

Set the mince balls aside to cool quickly and thoroughly. Put the mince balls and tomato sauce into six single-portion waxed cartons or into three double-portion ones. Seal, label, date and freeze.

To finish

Take the required quantity of mince balls and mixed vegetables from the freezer. Turn the mince balls and tomato sauce into a saucepan, heat gently and simmer for 15 minutes. Cook the vegetables in the usual way.

To serve

Serve the mince balls on a hot plate with the tomato sauce poured over. Sprinkle with crumbled frozen parsley and accompany with the hot mixed vegetables.

Steak in Redcurrant Sauce

From the freezer you have an excellent late meal for a minimum of effort.

Serves 6

3oz (75gm) butter
6 medium onions
¾ pint (375ml) beef stock
2 tablespoons redcurrant jelly
salt

black pepper
1oz (25gm) flour
6 frozen sirloin steaks
12 frozen croquette potatoes
1½lb (¾ kilo) frozen peas

To make Melt the butter in a frying pan. Peel and chop the onions and fry them until nicely brown. Add the stock, redcurrant jelly, salt and black pepper. Blend the flour with a little water and stir it gradually into the sauce to thicken it a little.

To freeze Cover the sauce and set it aside to cool quickly and thoroughly. Pour it into an ice cube tray then put the tray in the freezer. When frozen, turn the cubes into a polythene bag and spray with a little soda water to prevent them sticking together. Seal, label, date and return to the freezer.

To finish Take the required number of steaks from the freezer and allow them to thaw out slowly, if possible, before starting to fry them. If still frozen, start to fry them slowly. Take the required number of sauce cubes from the freezer and add to the steaks in the frying pan. Cook the steaks gently in the sauce until they are tender. Cook the frozen croquette potatoes and frozen peas in the usual way.

To serve Serve the steaks with the sauce poured over and accompanied with hot croquette potatoes and peas.

Seafood Casserole with Rice

Take this dish out of the freezer, pop it into the oven and, by the time you have had a quiet drink at the end of a busy day, your meal will be ready.

Serves 6

2lb (1 kilo) cod fillets
8oz (200gm) rice
1 can cream of lobster soup
8oz (200gm) frozen mushrooms
1 tablespoon lemon juice
salt

pepper
1 tablespoon tomato ketchup
4oz (100gm) frozen grated cheese
8oz (200gm) frozen peeled prawns
frozen parsley

To make Poach the cod in a little salted water, drain and break into chunks. Cook the rice in lightly salted, boiling water until it is almost tender, then drain and rinse well. Put all the remaining ingredients, except parsley, in a saucepan and heat gently, then add the cod chunks.

To freeze Put the rice into three greased, two-portion foil pie dishes and pour a third of the fish casserole over each. Cover the fish and set it aside to cool quickly and thoroughly. Seal, label, date and freeze.

To finish Take the required number of dishes of seafood casserole out of the freezer a few hours before required, if possible, and allow them to thaw out slowly in the refrigerator. Place on a baking sheet. Preheat the oven to moderate to moderately hot, 375 deg F or gas 5 (190 deg C) and put the casserole in the oven for 30 minutes to heat through.

To serve Remove the foil covers and put a few sprigs of parsley on top. Serve each casserole in its foil dish on a platter and with a green salad if liked.

Hot Fruit Salad and Cream

Quick and so easy – just the thing to complete a late meal.

Serves 6   ¾ pint (375ml) fresh double cream   ½ pint (250ml) sherry
2lb (1 kilo) frozen fruit salad

To make   Whip the cream until it is stiff and pipe six fairly big cream whirls on to a sheet of kitchen foil on a baking tray.

To freeze   Put the tray into the freezer. When the cream whirls are frozen, carefully remove them from the foil and pack them carefully in a plastic box. Seal, label, date and return to the freezer.

To finish   Take the required quantity of frozen fruit salad from the freezer and put it in a saucepan with a proportionate amount of sherry. Heat the fruit through very gently. Take the required number of cream whirls from the freezer.

To serve   Put the hot fruit salad in heatproof glass dishes, top each portion with a cream whirl and serve immediately.

Rhubarb Ice and Ginger Sauce

This is ideal for a late meal, as it is light and refreshing.

Serves 6   1½lb (¾ kilo) rhubarb   ½ pint (250ml) frozen double cream
1oz (25gm) butter   ¼ pint (125ml) frozen natural yogurt
4oz (100gm) caster sugar   1lb (½ kilo) ginger marmalade

To make   Wash and chop the rhubarb. Put it in a saucepan with the butter and sugar and stew it gently. When very soft, blend it to a purée in the blender or rub it through a hair sieve. Set it aside to cool completely. Meanwhile, take the cream and the yogurt from the freezer and allow them to thaw out almost completely. Beat the cream until it is fairly stiff, beat the yogurt and fold in the rhubarb purée.

To freeze   Put the rhubarb mixture into six single-size plastic moulds or empty yogurt cartons. Seal, label, date and freeze.

To finish   Put a tablespoon of ginger marmalade for each portion of rhubarb ice into a saucepan with a little water and heat it gently until the marmalade melts to give a smooth, pouring sauce. Take the required amount of rhubarb ice from the freezer.

To serve   Turn the rhubarb ice on to a glass dish and pour hot ginger sauce over the top. Serve immediately.

Feeding the family

A happy family is a well-fed family but what a trial it is at times to keep everyone happy and well-fed! Day in, day out, two or even three meals a day, seven days a week, fifty-two weeks a year . . . we all know the saga only too well. And much as we may love cooking, there comes a time when we need a rest to recharge the creative batteries if nothing else.

But how do you get a rest? Do you leave the family to it once in a while and take off on holiday? Or are you a conscientious Mum who would feel completely guilt-stricken if you were to do that?

Your freezer is your passport to freedom! Now you can salve your conscience by having a well-stocked freezer from which you can take the instant meal at a moment's notice. The family need never wait long for a meal, even if you have been out for the whole day or else too busy in the house to cope with cooking. You can even go away for a few days' break alone or with your husband and know that there is plenty in the freezer for those left behind.

Besides the freedom derived from owning a freezer, don't forget the sheer economy of it. Not only are you able to bulk buy foods in season and batch-cook them, thus saving time and money, leftovers can be frozen for future use or made up into other dishes and then frozen. Providing lunch for yourself and one youngster can take a considerable amount of time. Now that you have a freezer, you can cook lunch dishes in quantity, when you have the time, and freeze them in suitable amounts for quick service when needed.

I have chosen a selection of recipes which I'm sure you will find most useful in coping with the constant problem of what to give the family to eat.

Macaroni Soup

This is a slightly unusual soup that can be made in quantity and frozen for future use.

Serves 8

3 pints (1½ litres) water
3 chicken stock cubes
2lb (1 kilo) knuckle of veal
8oz (200gm) lean back bacon
3 medium onions
4 medium carrots
4 sticks celery

2 white turnips
rind of 2 lemons
sprig of thyme
peppercorns
3 blades of mace
8oz (200gm) macaroni
frozen parsley

To make

Bring 1½ pints (approximately ¾ litre) of the water to the boil in a large saucepan and blend in the stock cubes. Add the remaining water and the broken veal bones. (Ask the butcher to crush them for you.) Take the rind and most of the fat off the bacon, chop it up and add to the stock. Clean the vegetables, chop them up and add to the pan, together with the lemon rind, thyme, peppercorns and mace tied up in a little piece of muslin. Bring the stock slowly to the boil and let it simmer gently for 2 hours. Skim the froth off the top fairly often. Wash the macaroni. Strain the soup into a clean saucepan, bring it back to the boil and add the macaroni. Allow the soup to simmer for a further 15 minutes, or until the macaroni is almost tender.

To freeze

Turn the soup into a large basin, cover it with a light cloth and set it aside to cool quickly and thoroughly. Pour the soup into conveniently sized waxed cartons, seal, label, date and freeze.

To finish

Take the required quantity of soup out of the freezer and allow it to thaw out for a few hours at room temperature. Turn the soup into a saucepan and heat it slowly to boiling point. Simmer for 5 minutes.

To serve

Serve the soup piping hot in soup bowls with a little frozen parsley crumbled on the top.

Oxtail Soup

As this takes such a long time to cook, make it when you have a day on your own.

Serves 8

1 oxtail
2 large onions
2oz (50gm) butter
2oz (50gm) bacon
4 pints (approximately 2 litres)
   cold water
8oz (200gm) frozen stew pack
   vegetables

10 peppercorns
bouquet garni
2 cloves
salt
1oz (25gm) flour

To make

Wash the oxtail thoroughly and cut it into joints. Chop the onions. Melt the butter in a large saucepan and gently fry the onions. Chop the bacon and add it to the pan together with the oxtail joints. Fry them gently, then add the water, bring it to the boil and simmer the soup for 2 hours. Add the stew pack vegetables, peppercorns, bouquet garni, cloves and salt and simmer the soup for a further 2 hours. Strain the soup and thicken it with the flour blended with a little water.

To freeze

Turn the soup into a large basin, cover it with a light cloth and set it aside to cool quickly and thoroughly. Pour soup into waxed cartons, seal, label, date and freeze.

To finish

Take the required quantity of soup out of the freezer and allow it to thaw out a little at room temperature. Turn it into a saucepan and heat it through.

To serve

Serve the soup piping hot with fried croûtons.

Cheese and Bacon Crumb

Try this dish when unable to think of something tasty and light but different.

Serves 4

6oz (150gm) frozen grated cheese
1 tablespoon frozen chopped green
   pepper
2oz (50gm) frozen breadcrumbs
8oz (200gm) streaky bacon rashers

1 large onion
1oz (25gm) butter
8oz (200gm) frozen Brussels sprouts
8oz (200gm) tomato chutney

To make

Grease two two-portion, foil pie dishes. Mix together the cheese, green pepper and breadcrumbs and put a little of the mixture in the bottom of both pie dishes. Cut the rind off the bacon and chop the rashers. Divide half the bacon between the two dishes and spread it out over the cheese mixture. Chop the onion finely and fry it for 1–2 minutes in melted butter. Allow the Brussels sprouts to thaw out enough to enable you to chop them. Mix the onion with the chopped sprouts and divide half between the two pie dishes. Spread half the chutney into each pie dish, then add another layer of cheese mixture and a layer of the remaining onion mixture. Sprinkle the rest of the bacon on top, spread on the remaining chutney and finish with a layer of the remaining cheese mixture.

To freeze

Cover the pie dishes with kitchen foil, seal, label, date and freeze.

To finish

Preheat the oven to moderately hot, 400 deg F or gas 6 (200 deg C). Take the required number of dishes of Cheese and Bacon Crumb out of the freezer, uncover and place on a baking sheet. Put into the oven for 35–40 minutes to heat through thoroughly. If the top gets too brown, cover it lightly with a piece of kitchen foil.

To serve

Serve the Cheese and Bacon Crumb hot with a fresh green salad.

What could be easier than fish and chips (page 37) cooked straight from the freezer? And to follow, treat the family to the old favourite, bread and butter pudding (page 41).

Onion Pie

Try this onion pie for lunch on a really chilly day.

Serves 4

1 packet (4oz or 100gm) instant potato powder	8oz (200gm) onions
1 egg	salt
1oz (25gm) butter	pepper
milk	8oz (200gm) frozen grated cheese
8oz (200gm) tomatoes	2oz (50gm) frozen breadcrumbs

To make   Make up the instant potato according to the instructions on the packet but using slightly less water than directed. Beat the egg, half the butter and a little milk into the potato. Grease two two-portion, foil pie dishes and spread half the potato mixture in the bottom of each. Skin and slice the tomatoes and onions and arrange them in the pie dishes on top of the potato. Sprinkle with salt and pepper. Divide the cheese between the two pie dishes and top each with a layer of breadcrumbs. Dot each with the remaining butter.

To freeze   Cover each dish with kitchen foil, seal, label, date and freeze.

To finish   Preheat the oven to moderately hot, 400 deg F or gas 6 (200 deg C). Take the required number of dishes of Onion Pie out of the freezer and place on a baking sheet. Put into the oven for 10 minutes, then remove the cover and continue cooking for a further 25 minutes to heat thoroughly and brown and crisp the top.

To serve   Serve the pie hot with a green vegetable such as broccoli.

Kedgeree

This old favourite makes a tasty nourishing breakfast on which to send the family off for the day. And it doesn't take up valuable time in the morning.

Serves 8

2lb (1 kilo) frozen smoked haddock fillets	4oz (100gm) butter
1lb ($\frac{1}{2}$ kilo) rice	$\frac{1}{4}$ pint (125ml) tomato purée
salt	frozen parsley
pepper	$\frac{1}{2}$ pint (250ml) water

To make   Poach the frozen fish in water for 15 minutes, or until it is cooked. Drain and flake it. Cook the rice until it is almost tender in lightly salted, boiling water, then drain. In a large basin, mix together the fish and rice. Season the mixture with salt and pepper, stir in 3oz (75gm) of the butter and the tomato purée. Crumble in some frozen parsley.

To freeze   Cover the basin and set the kedgeree aside to cool quickly and thoroughly. Put the mixture into two four-portion polythene bags. Seal, label, date and freeze.

To finish   Take the required number of bags of kedgeree from the freezer. Use half the remaining ingredients to each bag of kedgeree, i.e. turn one bag of kedgeree into a large frying pan containing $\frac{1}{4}$ pint (125ml) boiling water and half the remaining butter. Simmer it gently for 15 minutes, or until the liquid is absorbed.

To serve   Serve the kedgeree on hot plates.

Fish and Chips

(Illustrated on page 35)

What could be easier than this, with the aid of a freezer?

Serves 4

4–8 frozen crumbed white fish
  fillets
2lb (1 kilo) frozen chips
1lb (½ kilo) frozen peas

deep fat for frying
1oz (25gm) butter
1 lemon
parsley

To make

Take the fish, chips and peas from the freezer. Heat the deep fat. From the frozen state, deep fry the fish fillets in faintly smoking hot fat until they are cooked through and golden brown. Transfer them to a dish and keep them warm in the oven. Clear any crumbs out of the fat and reheat it. Meanwhile, put the peas into a saucepan with a little lightly salted, boiling water and the butter. Cook gently. When the fat is faintly smoking hot, fry the chips from the frozen state until they are crisp and golden brown. Drain them on kitchen paper and pile them into a dish. Drain the peas and put them into a dish. Garnish the fish with lemon wedges and parsley sprigs.

To freeze

As everything comes from the freezer and is so quick to prepare, this section is not relevant.

To finish

The finishing of the dish is covered already as it is not frozen after cooking.

To serve

Serve fish and chips very hot as a main meal or as part of a high tea. Fried fish also makes a delicious breakfast dish.

Beef and Mushroom Stew

Every housewife is looking for something really nice but still economical to give her family. Try this warming dish.

Serves 8

3lb (1½ kilo) frozen shin of beef
2oz (50gm) flour
1 teaspoon ground ginger
salt
pepper
4oz (100gm) dripping
2 onions

2 sticks celery
2 teaspoons thyme
1 pint (approximately ½ litre)
  frozen beef stock
8oz (200gm) frozen sliced
  mushrooms

To make

Cut the meat into pieces. Mix together the flour, ginger, salt and pepper and toss the meat in it. Melt the dripping in a large saucepan and fry the meat to brown and seal it. Chop the onions and celery, add them to the pan and fry them gently. Add the thyme, then gradually stir in the stock. Cover and simmer gently for 1½ hours. Add the mushrooms to the stew.

To freeze

Line two casserole dishes with foil and turn the stew into them. Set them aside to cool quickly and thoroughly, then put in the freezer. When they are frozen, remove the dishes. Wrap the frozen stews in another layer of foil and put them in polythene bags. Seal, label, date and return to the freezer.

To finish

Preheat the oven to moderately hot, 400 deg F or gas 6 (200 deg C). Take the required quantity of stew from the freezer. Remove the polythene bag and outer layer of foil and put the frozen stew and foil into the relevant casserole. Cover it with foil and put it in the oven for 40 minutes to heat through thoroughly. Remove the foil and crumble frozen parsley over the top.

To serve

Serve the stew piping hot with boiled noodles and peas.

Veal Kidneys in Cream Sauce

Versatility is the word for this dish – it can be served as a main course, a supper snack or as a filling for cocktail savouries.

Serves 8

2oz (50gm) lard
1 bunch of spring onions
1lb (½ kilo) frozen button
  mushrooms
12 veal kidneys
1 pint (approximately ½ litre)
  frozen single cream

2oz (50gm) flour
½ pint (250ml) milk
⅛ pint (63ml) sherry
2 tablespoons made mustard
salt
pepper

To make

Melt the lard in a pan, chop the onions and fry them in the lard with the mushrooms and trimmed, chopped kidneys for 10 minutes. Take the mushrooms and kidneys out of the pan and keep on one side. Stir the cream into the juices and onion in the pan. Blend the flour with a little of the milk and mix it into the pan. Stir in the rest of the milk, the sherry, mustard, salt and pepper. Stir the sauce well until it thickens, then return the mushrooms and kidneys to the pan.

To freeze

Turn the mixture into conveniently sized foil dishes, cover with foil and set aside to cool quickly and thoroughly. Seal, label, date and freeze.

To finish

Preheat the oven to moderately hot, 400 deg F or gas 6 (200 deg C). Take the required number of dishes of kidneys out of the freezer and place on a baking sheet. Put into the oven for 30–35 minutes to heat through thoroughly.

To serve

Serve the Veal Kidneys in Cream Sauce hot with boiled rice and a green vegetable as a main course, on crisp toast for supper or in hot vol-au-vent cases as cocktail snacks.

Country Chicken Braise

Unusual flavours combine to make a delicious chicken dish.

Serves 8

8 frozen chicken joints
4oz (100gm) butter
2 small fennel
8oz (200gm) frozen sliced
  mushrooms
2 teaspoons tarragon

salt
pepper
1 pint (approximately ½ litre) cider
8 tomatoes, baked
2lb (1 kilo) frozen broccoli spears

To make

Take the chicken joints from the freezer and allow them to thaw out. Preheat the oven to very moderate, 325 deg F or gas 3 (170 deg C). Melt the butter in a frying pan and fry the chicken joints until the skin is crisp and brown. Slice the fennel and put it into the bottom of two greased large foil dishes. Divide the mushrooms between the two dishes. Lay four chicken joints on top of each dish and sprinkle with tarragon, salt and pepper. Pour the cider into the two dishes, cover them and place them on a baking sheet. Put in the oven and cook for 45 minutes.

To freeze

Set the chicken dishes aside to cool quickly and thoroughly. Seal, label, date and freeze.

To finish

Preheat the oven to moderately hot, 400 deg F or gas 6 (200 deg C). Take the required number of dishes of chicken out of the freezer and place on a baking sheet. Put into the oven for 35 minutes to heat through thoroughly.

To serve

Spoon the chicken out carefully on to a serving platter, pour the cider over and surround with baked tomatoes and cooked broccoli spears. Accompany with new potatoes.

Spare Ribs with Damson Sauce

Spare ribs have long been a favourite. Try them with this unusual fruit sauce.

Serves 8

16 spare rib pork chops
2lb (1 kilo) frozen stew pack
 vegetables
1 bayleaf
6 peppercorns
2 pints (approximately 1 litre)
 frozen ham stock

2lb (1 kilo) frozen damsons
2 tablespoons lemon juice
2oz (50gm) sugar
2oz (50gm) butter

To make

Put the pork chops into a saucepan and add the stew pack vegetables, bayleaf, peppercorns and ham stock. Bring to the boil and simmer gently for 1 hour, or until the meat is tender. Meanwhile, take the damsons from the freezer and put them in a saucepan with the lemon juice, sugar and butter. Simmer them gently until they are quite soft, then rub them through a hair sieve.

To freeze

Line two casserole dishes with foil and turn the stew into them. Cover and set them aside to cool quickly and thoroughly. Cool the damson purée, then pour it into empty yogurt cartons or waxed cartons. Seal, label, date and freeze the damson purée. Put the casseroles into the freezer and when they are frozen, remove the dish, wrap the solid stews in another layer of foil and place in polythene bags. Seal, label, date and return to the freezer.

To finish

Preheat the oven to moderately hot, 400 deg F or gas 6 (200 deg C). Take the required quantity of stew and damson purée out of the freezer. Take the stew out of the polythene bag and remove the outer layer of foil. Put it in the relevant casserole dish, cover it and place in the oven for 40 minutes to heat through thoroughly. Turn the required quantity of damson purée into a saucepan and heat through gently.

To serve

Spoon the meat out on to a serving dish and surround with the vegetables. Pour the damson sauce carefully over each chop. Garnish with crumbled frozen parsley and accompany with creamed potatoes.

Amber Lamb

Make the stuffing well in advance and store it in the freezer to save you time when you are preparing the Sunday lunch.

Serves 4

1 bunch of spring onions
8oz (200gm) frozen carrots
1oz (25gm) raisins
2 teaspoons crumbled frozen
 parsley
1 tablespoon frozen breadcrumbs

1oz (25gm) butter
salt
pepper
$\frac{1}{2}$ leg frozen lamb
$\frac{1}{4}$ pint (125ml) frozen lamb stock

To make

Chop the onions and cook them for 5 minutes in a little water. Meanwhile, take the carrots from the freezer and allow them to thaw out a little, then grate them finely. Drain the onions and mix them with the grated carrots, raisins, parsley, breadcrumbs, butter, salt and pepper.

To freeze

Put the stuffing into a polythene bag, seal, label, date and freeze.

To finish

Take the leg of lamb, stock and the stuffing out of the freezer the evening before they are required and allow them to thaw out at room temperature. Bone the lamb and pack the stuffing into the cavity. Tie the lamb together and put it in a roasting tin. Sprinkle it with salt and pepper, pour the stock round the joint, cover the tin and roast the joint in a moderate oven, 350 deg F or gas 4 (180 deg C) for $1\frac{1}{4}$ hours.

To serve

Serve the lamb with gravy, croquette potatoes, mixed vegetables and green beans.

Blackberry and Apple Crumble

Another family favourite that you can have any time of the year – thanks to your freezer.

Serves 8–10

2 packets (13½oz or 337gm) frozen shortcrust pastry
1lb (½ kilo) frozen blackberries
1lb (½ kilo) frozen apple slices
4oz (100gm) granulated sugar
6oz (150gm) butter
8oz (200gm) flour
2oz (50gm) demerara sugar

To make

Take the pastry from the freezer and allow it to thaw out sufficiently to enable you to roll it out. Preheat the oven to moderate to moderately hot, 375 deg F or gas 5 (190 deg C). Line two 10-inch (25cm) flan rings with the pastry. Take the fruits from the freezer and mix them with the granulated sugar. Divide the fruit between the two pastry cases. Press the fruit down slightly to make the surface flat. Rub the butter into the flour and mix in the demerara sugar. Spread this crumble mixture over the top of the two fruit flans, then bake the puddings in the oven for 40 minutes.

To freeze

The crumbles can either be frozen after putting them together and before cooking, or after cooking. I think it is better to cook them first before freezing. Set the cooked crumbles aside to cool quickly and thoroughly. Remove the flan rings and replace them with kitchen foil shaped round the base. Put the crumbles into polythene bags, seal, label, date and freeze.

To finish

If you want to eat the crumbles cold, take the required quantity from the freezer and allow them to thaw out for 2 hours at room temperature. Otherwise, preheat the oven to moderately hot, 400 deg F or gas 6 (200 deg C) and take the crumble from the freezer. Remove the polythene bag but not the foil base and place the crumble on a baking sheet. Put into the oven for 30 minutes to heat through thoroughly. You may need to cover the top lightly with a piece of foil to prevent it getting too brown.

To serve

Serve the Blackberry and Apple Crumble either hot or cold with cream.

Steamed Treacle Pudding

Why not have a couple of steamed puddings in the freezer ready for a cold day?

Serves 8

6oz (150gm) frozen chopped suet
1lb (½ kilo) flour
2 teaspoons ground ginger
salt
1 teaspoon baking soda
4oz (100gm) sugar
12oz (300gm) black treacle
2 eggs
½ pint (250ml) milk
1 pint (approximately ½ litre) water
2 lemons

To make

Take the suet from the freezer and turn it into a basin. Mix in the flour, ginger, a pinch of salt, the baking soda and sugar. In another small basin, mix together 4oz (100gm) of the treacle, the eggs and half the milk. Mix the liquids into the dry ingredients and add as much of the remaining milk as is necessary to form a soft consistency. Divide the mixture between two well-greased pudding basins, cover with greased kitchen foil and steam the puddings for 2½ hours.

To freeze

Turn the puddings out of the basins. Wrap them closely in kitchen foil and set them aside to cool quickly and thoroughly. Seal, label, date and freeze.

To finish

Take the required number of puddings from the freezer and steam them in their foil wrapping for 45 minutes–1 hour. To make the sauce, use half the remaining ingredients for each pudding, i.e. for each pudding, put 4oz (100gm) of the black treacle into a saucepan with half the water and the juice of 1 lemon. Bring to the boil and boil for 10 minutes. Take the pudding from the steamer, unwrap it and put it on a serving dish.

To serve

Serve the treacle pudding hot with the treacle sauce poured over or handed separately in a sauceboat. (This hot treacle sauce is also delicious poured over vanilla ice cream.)

Bread and Butter Pudding

(Illustrated on page 35)

Old-fashioned, perhaps, but still just as good. Think of that delicious sweet crisp topping!

Serves 8

1½ pints (approximately ¾ litre) milk
2 eggs
2oz (50gm) caster sugar

4oz (100gm) butter
4oz (100gm) white bread, thinly cut
3oz (75gm) currants
2oz (25gm) chopped peel

To make
Heat the milk gently. Whisk the eggs lightly and pour the warm milk over them. Stir in the sugar. Use a little of the butter to grease two conveniently sized foil pie dishes, and the rest to butter the bread slices. Cut the bread into smallish triangles, arrange them in the pie dishes and sprinkle throughout with currants and peel. Strain the custard over the bread, then set the pie dishes aside to let the custard soak into the bread. Preheat the oven to moderate to moderately hot, 375 deg F or gas 5 (190 deg C). Place the puddings on a baking sheet, put into the oven and bake for 30–40 minutes, or until they are brown and set.

To freeze
Set the puddings aside to cool quickly and thoroughly. Cover each pie dish with kitchen foil, seal, label, date and freeze.

To finish
Preheat the oven to moderate to moderately hot, 375 deg F or gas 5 (190 deg C). Take the required number of dishes of Bread and Butter Pudding out of the freezer and place, still covered, in a baking tin of warm water. Put into the oven for 40–45 minutes, to heat through thoroughly. Remove the cover 10 minutes before the end of cooking time to allow the top to crisp.

To serve
Although this is superb on its own, children sometimes like a spoonful of jam with it. Or make it more luxurious by serving it with cream.

Lemon Water Ice

Although there is an excellent range of ice cream and water ice on the market, it is sometimes rather nice to try your own special one. This is fantastic on a hot day.

Serves 8

4 pints (approximately 2 litres) water
16 lemons

2lb (1 kilo) granulated sugar
8 egg whites

To make
Put the water, grated rind of the lemons and the sugar into a pan. Bring it to the boil and boil rapidly until it is reduced to 1 pint (approximately ½ litre) syrup. Set it aside to cool quickly and thoroughly. Stir in the juice from the lemons.

To freeze
Pour the syrup into a large plastic container, such as an empty ice cream container, cover it and put it in the freezer. When it is half frozen, whisk the egg whites until just stiff and fold them into the iced lemon syrup. Re-cover the container, seal, label, date and return to the freezer.

To finish
Use the Lemon Water Ice direct from the freezer.

To serve
Eat it by itself or put a scoop on top of a slice of Swiss roll, pour cream over and sprinkle chopped, toasted almonds on top.

Working wives and mothers

Time is of the essence. Good management in the home and streamlining of the unavoidable tasks are the two main things that enable a working wife and mother to make a success of both her jobs. For, besides her responsibility to her employer, she has an even more important responsibility to make a loving and happy home for her husband and children. Therefore, she must be organised so that she has time to relax with the family. The main unavoidable task in any household is the cooking.

The freezer means you can shop in bulk even for perishables once a month, instead of spending your lunch hour in the supermarket. It also means you can buy more cheaply and cook in bulk, say, every second weekend to carry you through several days.

When it comes to entertaining, especially during the week, most working wives draw the line. But it need not be a time-consuming trial and, just to give you some ideas, I have included in this section two special meals which will delight your friends.

There are always the odd occasions when there's a rush job on and you have to work late or maybe you like to spend an evening, now and then, with the girls from the office. In both these cases, all you have to do is tell the family to help themselves to the stand-by meals that you have prepared ready in the freezer – all labelled with instructions on how to heat them for eating.

It's all a matter of organisation and "a little help from your friend", the freezer!

Cream of Spinach Soup

This soup is very simply made from your stock of food in the freezer.

Serves 6–8

1lb (½ kilo) frozen spinach
2 pints (approximately 1 litre) frozen chicken stock
1oz (25gm) butter

1oz (25gm) flour
1 pint (approximately ½ litre) milk
salt
pepper

To make — Put the frozen spinach with the frozen chicken stock into a large saucepan. Heat very slowly until they melt, then simmer for 30 minutes. Put the soup through the electric blender or rub it through a hair sieve and return it to the saucepan. In a small saucepan, melt the butter and add the flour. Remove the pan from the heat and gradually beat in half the milk. Return the pan to the heat and stir the mixture well to make a smooth sauce. Add some of the soup, then carefully pour the sauce into the soup, stirring constantly. Add salt and pepper to taste.

To freeze — Turn the soup into a basin, cover and set it aside to cool quickly and thoroughly. Pour it into conveniently sized waxed cartons, seal, label, date and freeze.

To finish — Take the required quantity of soup from the freezer, turn it into a saucepan and heat it gently to boiling point. Heat the proportionate amount of the remaining ½ pint (250ml) milk in a saucepan. Take the soup off the heat and stir in the hot milk.

To serve — Serve the soup in warmed soup bowls as a starter to a main meal or with hot, crusty bread and a piece of cheese for a quick, nourishing lunch or supper.

Despite the rush and hurry of a busy day at work, there's no need to deprive the family of those tasty dishes that would normally take such a long time to make. You can still give them beef in ale (page 45) and spotted dick with custard (page 48).

Beetroot Soup

The Russian name for this soup is Borsch and the recipe given here is my version of this Ukranian national soup.

Serves 6–8

3 large, raw beetroot
2 pints (approximately 1 litre) frozen beef stock
1 onion
4 cloves
bouquet garni
½ teaspoon caraway seeds
salt

pepper
1oz (25gm) bacon fat
8oz (200gm) mixture of shredded celery, white cabbage and raw beetroot
¼ pint (125ml) soured cream
milk

To make

Wash the beetroot thoroughly and slice them. Put them into a large saucepan with the stock, onion stuck with the cloves, bouquet garni and caraway seeds. Bring slowly to the boil and simmer for 1 hour. Strain the soup into a basin, season, then set it aside to cool. Meanwhile, melt the bacon fat in a pan and gently fry the shredded vegetables for 10–15 minutes. Add the vegetables to the cooling soup.

To freeze

When the soup is thoroughly cold, pour it into conveniently sized waxed cartons. Seal, label, date and freeze.

To finish

Take the required quantity of soup from the freezer, turn it into a saucepan and heat it gently to boiling point. Thin the proportionate amount of soured cream down very slightly with a little milk. Pour the soup into soup bowls and top each with a spoonful of soured cream.

To serve

Although the soured cream is essential to the correct version of Borsch, some people may not like it. In this case, put the soured cream in a small dish and hand it separately.

Creole Baked Halibut

Fish freezes beautifully, so try this for the family meal. They will love it.

Serves 8

8 frozen halibut steaks
1 onion
2 frozen green sweet peppers
2 frozen red sweet peppers
¾ pint (375ml) frozen tomato purée

salt
pepper
3oz (75gm) frozen grated cheese
frozen parsley
2 tomatoes

To make

Take all the necessary ingredients from the freezer except the parsley. Poach the halibut steaks in a little water for 10 minutes to cook them partly. Drain the fish and divide it between two greased foil dishes. Chop the onion and peppers finely and mix them with the tomato purée, salt, pepper and cheese. Pour this mixture over the fish in the two dishes.

To freeze

Cover the dishes with greased kitchen foil. Seal, label, date and freeze.

To finish

Preheat the oven to moderately hot, 400 deg F or gas 6 (200 deg C). Take the required number of dishes of halibut out of the freezer and place on a baking sheet. Put into the oven for 45 minutes to finish cooking the fish and heat the sauce.

To serve

Lift the halibut steaks on to a serving platter, pour the sauce over and garnish with parsley sprigs and sliced tomatoes. Serve with creamed potatoes, peas and sweetcorn.

Beef in Ale
(Illustrated on page 43)

Cook this dish when you have time and then freeze it ready to use at short notice.

Serves 6–8

2½lb (1¼ kilo) frozen silverside of beef
½ pint (250ml) brown ale
1 tablespoon vinegar
2 bayleaves
pinch of allspice
1½lb (¾ kilo) frozen stew pack vegetables

salt
pepper
½oz (12gm) flour
2 cartons soured cream
parsley

To make

Take the beef from the freezer and put it straight into a large saucepan with all the remaining ingredients except the flour, soured cream and parsley. Bring to the boil, cover the pan and simmer for 2½ hours. Lift the meat out and carve it into slices. Put it into two large, shallow foil dishes. Strain the liquid and make it up to ¾ pint (375ml) with water. Thicken the liquid slightly with the flour blended with a little water, then pour over the meat in the two dishes.

To freeze

Cover the foil dishes with greased kitchen foil and set aside to cool quickly and thoroughly. Seal, label, date and freeze.

To finish

Preheat the oven to moderate to moderately hot, 375 deg F or gas 5 (190 deg C). Take the required number of dishes of beef out of the freezer and place on a baking sheet. Put into the oven for 35 minutes to heat through thoroughly. Uncover each dish and lift the meat and gravy out on to a warm dish. Spoon soured cream over the meat.

To serve

Serve the Beef in Ale hot, garnished with parsley. Accompany with creamed potatoes and mixed vegetables.

Crispy Turkey Pancakes

Savoury pancakes take quite a time to make but they freeze excellently, thus saving a lot of time.

Serves 8

1 pint (approximately ½ litre) frozen pancake batter (see lemon pancakes, page 76)
½ pint (250ml) frozen béchamel sauce (see page 59)

1lb (½ kilo) cooked turkey meat
2 teaspoons hot curry powder
¼ pint (125ml) soured cream
4oz (100gm) frozen grated cheese

To make

Take the batter and the béchamel sauce from the freezer and allow them to thaw out. Make 16 pancakes from the batter. Chop the turkey meat in small dice and mix it into the sauce. Mix the curry powder with the soured cream and stir it into the turkey mixture. Spoon some mixture into each of the 16 pancakes and roll them up.

To freeze

Put eight filled pancakes in each of two well greased foil dishes. Cover the dishes with greased kitchen foil. Seal, label, date and freeze.

To finish

Preheat the oven to moderate to moderately hot, 375 deg F or gas 5 (190 deg C). Take the required number of dishes of pancakes out of the freezer and place on a baking sheet. Put into the oven for 30 minutes to heat through thoroughly. Remove the cover and sprinkle the top of each dish with 2oz (50gm) of the cheese. Place under a hot grill to melt, brown and crisp the top.

To serve

Put the foil dish on to a platter. Serve the pancakes from the dish and accompany each serving with a tomato, peas and onion salad.

Ox Heart Dumpling

Although the suet pastry is being used here for a savoury dumpling, the same pastry is delicious with a filling of almost any fruit from your freezer, especially apples and blackberries.

Serves 8–10

12oz (300gm) frozen shoulder steak
2lb (1 kilo) frozen ox heart
1lb ($\frac{1}{2}$ kilo) flour
8oz (200gm) finely chopped suet
1 teaspoon salt
3–4 teaspoons baking powder

about $\frac{1}{4}$ pint (125ml) water
4 onions
1 teaspoon sage
1 teaspoon basil
salt
pepper

To make

Take the meats from the freezer and allow them to thaw out enough to enable you to cut them. Mix together the flour, suet, salt and baking powder. Then work in sufficient of the water to give an elastic dough. Turn it out on to a floured board. Divide it in half and roll each piece out to a round about $\frac{1}{4}$–$\frac{1}{2}$ inch thick. Cut out a quarter of each circle and use the rest to line two foil-lined, well greased pudding basins. Seal the joins in the suet pastry with water. Chop the meats and the onions and mix them together with the sage, basil, salt and pepper. Put half of the meat mixture into each pudding basin and pour over a little water. Roll out the remaining pastry into two circles to form lids for the dumplings. Seal the edges tightly, cover with greased kitchen foil and steam for $2\frac{1}{2}$ hours.

To freeze

Let the dumplings cool in the basins then turn them out, still keeping the covering of foil on them. Wrap each again closely in another layer of kitchen foil. Seal, label, date and freeze.

To finish

Take the required number of dumplings out of the freezer and remove the outer wrapping of foil. Make sure the top is covered closely with greased foil and put each pudding into the top half of a steamer for 50 minutes–1 hour to heat through thoroughly. Turn each dumpling on to a warm serving platter, carefully remove the foil and put a sprig of parsley on top.

To serve

Serve the Ox Heart Dumpling with plenty of buttered green beans and onions in white sauce. (If you decide to make a fruit dumpling, you need only steam it for 1 hour before freezing and for 40 minutes after freezing. Serve it with cream or custard.)

Coffee Pudding

There is no need to stick to fruit and ice cream for the dessert. Make this and put it in the freezer ready to use whenever you want.

Serves 8

4 eggs
8oz (200gm) caster sugar
5oz (125gm) flour
2lb (1 kilo) icing sugar
5 tablespoons strong black coffee

8oz (200gm) butter
2 teaspoons coffee essence
1 pint (approximately ½ litre)
  frozen double cream

To make

Preheat the oven to very moderate, 325 deg F or gas 3 (170 deg C). Lightly grease two ring moulds. Put the eggs and sugar into a basin and whisk them over a pan of hot water until they are thick and creamy. Alternatively, use an electric whisk, in which case there is no need to put the mixture over hot water. Sift the flour and fold it into the eggs and sugar mixture. Divide the mixture between the two moulds and bake them in the oven for 45 minutes, or until the puddings are set and pale golden. Turn the puddings out on to a wire tray and let them cool. Mix half the icing sugar with the black coffee and coat the two puddings with this. Soften the butter and mix in the remaining icing sugar and the coffee essence. Put this into a piping bag. When the icing on the puddings is set, carefully lift each pudding on to a suitably sized cake board and decorate the tops and edges with the coffee butter icing. Let the frozen double cream thaw a little, then whip it until it is stiff. Put it into a piping bag and pipe the cream into the centre of each pudding.

To freeze

Place the puddings, on their boards, in the freezer. When they are frozen, put each one carefully in a box to protect the cream decoration from getting knocked and broken. Alternatively, wrap each pudding in a large polythene bag or in a double layer of cling film. Seal, label, date and return them to the freezer.

To finish

Take the required number of puddings out of the freezer in the morning before you go to work. Remove the wrappings and leave to thaw out at room temperature. There is no more finishing needed, beyond putting each pudding on a plate and on to the table.

To serve

Serve the pudding cold either by itself or with some fruit from the freezer.

Ham and Broad Beans

If one of the family wants an early meal before going out for the evening, he can help himself to this out of the freezer.

Serves 4

1lb (½ kilo) cooked ham
½ pint (250ml) frozen béchamel
  sauce (see page 59)
1lb (½ kilo) frozen broad beans

2 tablespoons crumbled frozen
  parsley
8 frozen croquette potatoes

To make

Cut the ham into dice. Take the béchamel sauce from the freezer and allow it to thaw out at room temperature. Mix the ham, frozen beans and parsley into the sauce. Put the mixture into four greased, single-size foil dishes and put two frozen croquette potatoes on each dish.

To freeze

Cover each dish with foil. Seal, label, date and freeze. It is a good idea to put brief finishing and serving instructions on the label if other members of the family are going to be helping themselves.

To finish

Preheat the oven to moderately hot, 400 deg F or gas 6 (200 deg C). Take the required number of dishes out of the freezer and place them on a baking sheet. Put them in the oven for 35 minutes to heat through thoroughly.

To serve

Uncover each foil dish and serve the Ham and Broad Beans on to warm plates.

Kidney Crisp

Held up late at work? Phone the family and tell them to help themselves to this dish.

Serves 4

2 tablespoons olive oil
1oz (25gm) butter
1lb (½ kilo) frozen lamb's kidneys
8oz (200gm) frozen fried, sliced
   mushrooms
2 onions
salt

cayenne pepper
¼ pint (125ml) frozen tomato purée
1lb (½ kilo) potatoes, peeled and
   thinly sliced
deep fat for frying
3oz (75gm) frozen grated cheese

To make

Heat the oil and butter in a pan and gently fry the trimmed and chopped kidneys, the mushrooms and chopped onions until they are tender. Season the mixture with salt and a little cayenne pepper, then turn it into a well greased, deep foil pie dish. Spread the tomato purée over the top. Deep fry the potato slices until they are crisp and golden. Cover the kidney with the potato slices and sprinkle the grated cheese over.

To freeze

Cover the dish with greased kitchen foil and set aside to cool quickly and thoroughly. Seal, label, date and freeze. Here again, it is a good idea to put brief finishing and serving instructions on the label.

To finish

Preheat the oven to moderate to moderately hot, 375 deg F or gas 5 (190 deg C). Take the Kidney Crisp out of the freezer and place it on a baking sheet. Put into the oven for 30 minutes to heat through thoroughly. Remove the cover, turn the oven temperature up to moderately hot, 400 deg F or gas 6 (200 deg C) and cook for a further 10 minutes to crisp the cheese topping.

To serve

Serve this direct from the dish on to warm plates. It is a meal in itself but sweetcorn goes well with it if you want an accompanying vegetable.

Spotted Dick
(*Illustrated on page 43*)

Does this raise memories of your own childhood? Introduce your youngsters to it.

Serves 8–10

1lb (½ kilo) flour
3 teaspoons baking powder
8oz (200gm) butter
6oz (150gm) sugar

4 eggs
milk
8oz (200gm) currants

To make

Sift the flour and baking powder into a basin. Rub in the butter until the mixture resembles fine breadcrumbs, then mix in the sugar. Beat the eggs and mix them with the dry ingredients, together with sufficient milk to make a dropping consistency. Mix in the currants and divide the mixture between two foil-lined, greased pudding basins. Cover the basins with greased kitchen foil and steam the puddings for 1½ hours.

To freeze

Uncover the puddings and take them, still in their foil wrapping, out of the basins and set them aside to cool quickly and thoroughly. Wrap the puddings in another layer of kitchen foil, seal, label, date and freeze.

To finish

Take the required number of puddings out of the freezer before you go to work and leave to thaw out at room temperature. Take the outer layer of foil off each pudding and cover the top with a small piece of foil. Make sure it is sealed well, then put the pudding into the top half of the steamer and steam for 30 minutes to heat through thoroughly. Take it out, unwrap it and turn it on to a serving dish.

To serve

Cut the pudding in wedges to serve. Custard sauce is traditional with Spotted Dick, though cream is also delicious.

Pumpkin Soup

Pumpkin is still rather unusual in Britain, so try this soup as something special.

Serves 6–8

1oz (25gm) butter
2 onions
1lb (½ kilo) peeled pumpkin
1oz (25gm) split peas
3 pints (approximately 1½ litres)
   frozen chicken stock

celery leaves
½ teaspoon thyme
salt
pepper
2 teaspoons crumbled frozen
   parsley

To make

Melt the butter in a large saucepan. Peel and slice the onions and fry them in the butter until they are soft but not browned. Cut the pumpkin in pieces and add it, together with all the remaining ingredients except the parsley, to the saucepan. Bring the soup to the boil and simmer it for 1 hour. Strain the soup into a basin and rub the vegetables through a hair sieve.

To freeze

Set the soup aside to cool quickly and thoroughly. Pour it into conveniently sized waxed cartons, seal, label, date and freeze.

To finish

Take the required quantity of soup from the freezer and let it thaw out a little. Turn it into a saucepan and heat it gently to boiling point. Sprinkle in crumbled frozen parsley.

To serve

Serve the soup in soup bowls and accompany with bread rolls from the freezer. Stir a spoonful of single cream into each portion of soup, if liked.

Lamb Curls

Having good quality frozen meat in the freezer saves the working wife so much time, especially when she wants something for a rather special meal.

Serves 8

8 large frozen loin of lamb chops
8 frozen sheep's kidneys
8 streaky bacon rashers
pepper
1 teaspoon powdered rosemary

¼ pint (125ml) Madeira wine
1 pint (approximately ½ litre)
   Madeira sauce (see page 59)
2oz (50gm) dripping
frozen parsley

To make

Take the meat from the freezer and allow it to thaw out for 36 hours at room temperature. The evening before you are going to cook the meat, remove the bones from the chops, and bend each round to enclose a kidney. Stretch the bacon rashers with the back of the knife and wind a rasher round each chop to hold it together. Rub pepper and rosemary into the surface of each and put the chops to marinate in the Madeira wine. Leave them in the refrigerator until you are ready to cook them the next evening.

To freeze

Freezing this dish at this stage does not serve any purpose. Having the ingredients in the freezer is enough to enable you to make Lamb Curls with the minimum amount of effort.

To finish

Take the Madeira sauce from the freezer and heat it gently. Lift the chops out of the marinade and place in the grill pan. Pour the marinade into the Madeira sauce. Dot the surface of each chop with dripping and put them under a hot grill to cook.

To serve

Put the Lamb Curls on a serving platter, garnish with parsley and accompany with new potatoes and ratatouille. Hand the Madeira sauce separately, in a sauceboat.

Bramble Bombe

A little last-minute attention is required for this gorgeous dessert but your guests will think it well worth it.

Serves 6–8

½ pint (250ml) home-frozen blackberry purée
½ pint (250ml) frozen double cream
caster sugar to taste
¼ pint (125ml) natural yogurt
few whole frozen blackberries for decoration

7-inch (18cm) frozen plain sponge cake
4oz (100gm) apple jelly
2 egg whites
3oz (75gm) caster sugar

To make Allow the purée and the cream to thaw out. Mix caster sugar to taste into the blackberry purée and whip the cream. Whip the yogurt into the cream and fold in the purée.

To freeze Put a polythene bag into a 1-pint (approximately ½-litre) basin and pour the blackberry cream into it. Put it into the freezer and when it is frozen, remove the bag from the basin. Seal, label, date and return the bag to the freezer.

To finish Take some whole frozen blackberries from the freezer and allow them to thaw out on a piece of kitchen paper. Take the plain sponge cake from the freezer and allow it to thaw out almost completely. Spread the cake with the apple jelly. When the dessert is required, preheat the oven to moderately hot, 400 deg F or gas 6 (200 deg C). Whisk up the egg whites and beat in the sugar to make a meringue mixture. Put the sponge on an ovenproof plate. Take the frozen blackberry cream from the freezer, unwrap it and put it on top of the sponge. Cover the blackberry cream completely, carefully and quickly with the meringue mixture and pop it into the oven for a few minutes to set and brown the meringue.

To serve Decorate the top with the whole blackberries and serve immediately.

Chilled Sweet Pepper Soup

This is a delicious starter to a special meal on a warm evening.

Serves 6–8

2oz (50gm) butter
1 onion
1 small frozen green sweet pepper
1 small frozen red sweet pepper
1 pint (approximately ½ litre) frozen jellied consommé (see page 90)

1 pint (approximately ½ litre) milk
½ pint (250ml) frozen single cream
salt
pepper

To make Take everything you need from the freezer. Melt the butter in a large saucepan. Chop the onion and the peppers finely and fry them gently in the butter to soften but not brown them. Add the consommé and simmer the mixture for 15 minutes. Set it aside to cool. Stir in the milk and cream. Season the soup with salt and pepper and put it in the refrigerator to chill.

To freeze As this soup is so simple and quick to make there is little point in freezing it.

To finish Stir the chilled soup well and pour into glass bowls set in slightly larger bowls filled with chipped ice cubes.

To serve Serve the chilled soup as a starter, accompanied with brown bread and butter.

Prawn Thermidor

A delicious new way with prawns that can be made so quickly – thanks to the freezer.

Serves 6

½ pint (250ml) frozen béchamel
   sauce (see page 59)
¼ pint (125ml) frozen single cream
1 tablespoon vinegar
1 teaspoon made mustard
4oz (100gm) frozen, fried, sliced
   mushrooms

1½lb (¾ kilo) frozen prawns
8oz (200gm) rice
4oz (100gm) frozen grated cheese
2 lemons
frozen parsley

To make

Take everything you need from the freezer. Turn the béchamel sauce into a saucepan and heat it gently. Add all the remaining ingredients except the rice, 1oz (25gm) of the cheese, the lemons and parsley. Heat them very gently but thoroughly. Meanwhile, boil the rice in the usual way, drain it and put it on to a large ovenproof serving dish. Pour the prawn mixture into the centre of the rice, sprinkle the remaining grated cheese on top and melt and brown the top under a hot grill.

To freeze

As this dish is so quick to make, there is no real advantage in freezing.

To finish

Garnish the dish with lemon curls and parsley.

To serve

Serve the Prawn Thermidor piping hot, accompanied with a fresh green salad.

Raspberry Gâteau

Guests always seem to appear when you are up to your ears in work. Don't panic – let the freezer take the strain. Try this for a quick but elegant dessert.

Serves 6–8

2 frozen chocolate cakes
   (see page 68)
¼ pint (125ml) sherry
1lb (½ kilo) frozen raspberries
1 pint (approximately ½ litre) frozen
   double cream

4oz (100gm) frozen grated
   chocolate
2oz (50gm) flaked almonds

To make

Take everything you need from the freezer and allow them to thaw out for about 1 hour. Split the two cakes and sprinkle each half with sherry. Put aside a few whole raspberries for decoration and mash the rest very slightly. Spread each half of cake on one side with the mashed raspberry. Whip the cream until it is stiff and, using half of it, spread three of the cake halves with it on top of the raspberry purée. Sandwich the halves together so that the one with no cream on it is on top. Use the remaining cream to coat the sides of the cake and to decorate round the top edge. Press grated chocolate on to the cream on the sides and then stick on the almond flakes. Decorate the top with the reserved whole raspberries.

To freeze

Put the gâteau on a cake board and put it in the freezer. When it is frozen hard, put it in a box, a large polythene bag or in a double layer of cling film. Seal, label, date and return it to the freezer.

To finish

Take the gâteau from the freezer in the morning before you leave for work, take the wrappings off and let it thaw out at room temperature. There is no other finishing needed, beyond putting it on a plate and taking it to the table.

To serve

Serve this sumptuous gâteau as a dessert on a special occasion.

Sharp Chicken Sandwich Filling

Someone in the family is sure to decide at the last moment that he wants sandwiches for lunch. Have a reserve of fillings in the freezer such as this one. It is also an excellent way of using up very small scraps of chicken.

Makes about 9oz (225gm)

6oz (150gm) cooked chicken scraps
2oz (50gm) butter
2 teaspoons anchovy essence

cayenne pepper
1 tablespoon mango chutney
salt

To make Shred the chicken very finely and work in the butter. Add the anchovy essence, cayenne pepper to taste and the chutney. It probably will not need any salt but taste the filling to make sure.

To freeze Pack the filling into small, empty cream cartons. Seal, label, date and freeze.

To finish Take the filling from the freezer 40 minutes before you need it, to allow it to thaw sufficiently for spreading.

To serve This sandwich filling is delicious spread on crispbread or cheese biscuits for cocktail savouries.

Salmon and Watercress Sandwich Filling

Don't waste those very tiny bits of that delicious salmon (see page 86). Pick over the skin and the bone carefully and use them to make this sandwich filling.

Makes about 4oz (100gm)

3oz (75gm) cooked salmon scraps
few watercress leaves

1 tablespoon soured cream
black pepper

To make Put the salmon into a basin and mash it with a fork. Chop the watercress leaves very finely and mix them into the salmon. Add the soured cream and black pepper to taste.

To freeze Pack the filling into small, empty cream cartons. Seal, label, date and freeze.

To finish Take the filling from the freezer 40 minutes before you need it, to allow it to thaw sufficiently for spreading.

To serve This filling is at its best spread on buttered brown bread.

Holidays

For Mum holiday means one thing. It is the time when the children are at home all the time and Mum is expected to provide super, special meals for far more people than she ever does normally. Yet she is still expected to be one of the family. She is expected to be available to go on picnics; to listen to the new record player the children got for Christmas; to rescue young Peter who's got stuck up a tree; to trail round museums; and, as if all that wasn't enough, she is expected to sit down to dinner with her husband as if she had spent all day doing nothing. Holiday for Mum is spelt CHAOS!

Or it used to be spelt that way but it need not be any longer. Plan and cook as much as you can well in advance when you have peace and quiet and the house to yourself. Put everything in the freezer and then you, too, can relax and enjoy having the family at home. It is so simple to take ready-made dishes from the freezer and heat them up, that you may find the children can cope with the odd meal and you can have a day off.

Besides using the freezer to make life easier for yourself, it means that the family can have some of those special things that they love but that used to take time to prepare. The very essence of a holiday is that it is a relaxed time when there are no time-tables to be adhered to and life is played by ear. It may dawn a beautiful day and the children decide to go off on a long bicycle run into the country. They want a picnic lunch – it's in the freezer. Or you have all got back late from a shopping spree but you still want a quick, out-of-the-ordinary meal. Make use of one of the super sauces in the freezer. It's always hectic getting everyone organised, packed and in the car, leaving the house cleaned and shut to go away on holiday. But at least the picnic lunch was prepared weeks ago and is all ready in the freezer.

Included in this section are a few Christmas recipes too but, in fact, any of the recipes throughout the book will help alleviate holiday chaos.

Cheesy Chicken Drumsticks
(Illustrated on page 55)

Chicken drumsticks are so easy to eat that they are a natural for a picnic as a change from sandwiches. They also provide a simple and nourishing meal on a long car journey.

Serves 8	8 frozen chicken drumsticks	pepper
	4oz (100gm) frozen breadcrumbs	2oz (50gm) flour
	2oz (50gm) frozen grated cheese	1 egg
	2 teaspoons sage	milk
	salt	deep fat for frying

To make — Take the chicken drumsticks from the freezer and allow them to thaw out. Mix together the breadcrumbs, cheese and sage. Mix salt and pepper into the flour and coat the thawed drumsticks in this, then dip them in the egg beaten with a little milk. Coat the drumsticks carefully in the breadcrumb mixture. Repeat this process so that the chicken drumsticks are coated in egg and crumbs twice. Deep fry the drumsticks in faintly smoking hot fat for about 10 minutes, or until the chicken is cooked through and the coating crisp and golden. Drain them on kitchen paper.

To freeze — Set the drumsticks aside to cool quickly and thoroughly. Pack them carefully in a plastic box. Seal, label, date and freeze.

To finish — Take the required quantity of drumsticks out of the freezer the evening before your picnic and let them thaw out at room temperature.

To serve — Serve the drumsticks cold with crisp lettuce and fresh tomatoes.

Ayrshire Pies

These tasty pies are ideal for a picnic or a snack lunch at home.

Serves 8–10

12oz (300gm) flour
1 teaspoon salt
4oz (100gm) lard
¼ pint (125ml) milk
12oz (300gm) cold, cooked lamb

4oz (100gm) lamb's liver
1 small onion
2 teaspoons mixed spice
salt
black pepper

To make

Mix the flour and 1 teaspoon salt together in a basin. Put the lard and milk in a saucepan and bring them to the boil. Pour the liquid into the flour and work it together to form a smooth dough. Cover the basin and keep it warm. Let it stand for 10 minutes. Preheat the oven to hot, 425 deg F or gas 7 (220 deg C). Mince together the lamb, liver and onion and mix in the spice, salt and pepper. Add a little water if the mixture is rather dry. Working quickly, roll the pastry out very thinly and cut 8–10 circles the size of a saucer and the same number of circles slightly larger than the base of a jam jar. Work each of the larger pastry circles up round the greased base of a jam jar to make pastry cups. Put some meat mixture in each and use the smaller circles of pastry to form a lid for each pie. Seal the edges and make a small hole in the middle of each lid. Bake the pies in the oven for 10 minutes to set the pastry and then reduce the oven temperature to moderate, 350 deg F or gas 4 (180 deg C) and bake for a further 20 minutes.

To freeze

Cool the pies on a wire cooling tray, then pack them in convenient quantities in polythene bags. Seal, label, date and freeze.

To finish

Take pies from the freezer and thaw out at room temperature. If you want to eat the pies hot, unwrap them and place them on a baking sheet. Put them into the oven preheated to moderately hot, 400 deg F or gas 6 (200 deg C) for 30 minutes to heat through.

To serve

Serve the pies cold with a salad for a picnic or hot with baked beans for a snack lunch.

Savoury Egg Flan

(*Illustrated opposite*)

Make at least two of these and keep them in the freezer as useful stand-bys.

Serves 8–10

1 packet (13½oz or 337gm) frozen
   shortcrust pastry
8oz (200gm) back bacon rashers
4oz (100gm) onion, grated
4oz (100gm) frozen grated cheese

4 eggs
¾ pint (375ml) milk
salt
pepper

To make

Take the pastry from the freezer and allow it to thaw out sufficiently to enable you to roll it out. Preheat the oven to moderately hot, 400 deg F or gas 6 (200 deg C). Line two foil pie dishes, 1 inch (2·5cm) deep by 9 inches (22cm) diameter, with the pastry and bake them blind. Let the pastry flans cool. Reduce the oven temperature to moderate to moderately hot, 375 deg F or gas 5 (190 deg C). Meanwhile, chop the bacon and mix it together with all the remaining ingredients. Pour the mixture into each of the two flans and bake them in the oven for 30–35 minutes.

To freeze

Set the flans aside to cool quickly and thoroughly, then wrap each in a polythene bag. Seal, label, date and freeze.

To finish

Take flans out of the freezer and thaw out for a few hours at room temperature.

To serve

Serve the flan cold with salad for a main meal or take one on a picnic.

Cheesy chicken drumsticks (page 53) and savoury egg flan (above) are ideal for a picnic, with the addition of fruit and frozen gâteau.

Minty Pork Loaf

Everyone has a special favourite meat loaf recipe. This is mine.

Serves 10–12

3lb (1½ kilo) frozen minced shoulder pork
8oz (200gm) frozen mushrooms
1 bunch of spring onions
2 tablespoons crumbled frozen mint
½ pint (250ml) frozen chicken stock
salt
pepper
1 tablespoon lemon juice
2 hard-boiled eggs
1 egg
1 egg yolk
thinly cut bacon rashers

To make

Take the meat and the mushrooms from the freezer and allow them to thaw out a little. Chop the mushrooms and the onions and put all the ingredients except the eggs and the bacon rashers into a saucepan. Cook gently for 20 minutes. Preheat the oven to moderate to moderately hot, 375 deg F or gas 5 (190 deg C). Chop the hard-boiled eggs and add them to the pan. Beat the whole egg and the egg yolk into the warm mixture. Line two 1lb (½-kilo) loaf tins carefully with kitchen foil, then with the bacon rashers and divide the meat between the two tins. Cover the tins with foil and bake them in the oven for 1 hour.

To freeze

Set the meat loaves aside to cool quickly and thoroughly in the tins, then turn them out and wrap each in another layer of foil. Seal, label, date and freeze.

To finish

Take the required number of loaves out of the freezer the day before they are needed and allow them to thaw out in the refrigerator. Unwrap each meat loaf and turn it on to a serving platter.

To serve

Cut the meat into slices and serve with a salad or hot vegetables.

Spiced Apple Tarts

Make large, individual fruit pies when you have time, so there is always a dessert on hand.

Serves 8

2 packets (13½oz or 337gm) frozen shortcrust pastry
2lb (1 kilo) frozen apple slices
2 teaspoons ground cloves
4oz (100gm) demerara sugar
oil

To make

Take the pastry from the freezer and allow it to thaw out sufficiently to enable you to roll it. Line eight foil dishes with pastry reserving enough for the lids, and pack in frozen apple slices. Sprinkle each with a mixture of cloves and sugar. Cut pastry lids, brush one side with oil and cover the tarts with the lids, oil side down. Seal the edges.

To freeze

Put the tarts into the freezer and, when they are frozen, pack them carefully in plastic boxes. Seal, label, date and freeze.

To finish

Preheat the oven to hot, 425 deg F or gas 7 (220 deg C). Take the required number of tarts out of the freezer and bake them in the oven for 35–40 minutes.

To serve

Serve the tarts hot with custard or cream for a meal at home, or cold as a delicious addition to a picnic meal.

Mince Pies

Make your own delicious mincemeat to fill these traditionally Christmas pies.

Makes 24–30

8oz (200gm) frozen apple slices
4oz (100gm) finely chopped suet
4oz (100gm) raisins
3oz (75gm) chopped mixed peel
1oz (25gm) chopped almonds
1 tablespoon grated lemon rind
3oz (75gm) soft brown sugar

½ teaspoon salt
2 teaspoons mixed spice
¼ pint (125ml) brandy
2 packets (13½oz or 337gm)
  frozen puff pastry
1 egg

To make
Take the apple slices from the freezer and allow them to thaw sufficiently to enable you to chop them. Mix the apple with all the remaining ingredients except the puff pastry and the egg. Pack the mincemeat into jars, cover and set aside to use when needed. It will keep for several months. Take the pastry from the freezer and allow it to thaw out sufficiently to enable you to roll it out thinly. Cut the pastry in circles and line small foil patty tins, reserving enough pastry to make lids for each pie. Put a spoonful of mincemeat in each pastry case and cover with a pastry lid. Seal the edges.

To freeze
Set the uncooked pies on a tray and put them in the freezer. When they are frozen, pack them into plastic boxes. Seal, label, date and return to the freezer.

To finish
Preheat the oven to hot, 425 deg F or gas 7 (220 deg C). Take the required number of pies from the freezer, brush the tops with beaten egg and place them on a baking sheet. Put into the oven for 15 minutes to set the pastry, then reduce the oven temperature to moderate to moderately hot, 375 deg F or gas 5 (190 deg C) and bake the pies for a further 15 minutes.

To serve
Serve the Mince Pies hot with brandy sauce (see page 60), custard or cream as a dessert, or cold for tea or as part of a snack meal.

Chestnut Stuffing

Save time in the Christmas rush – make this stuffing in advance and freeze it.

Makes about
2lb (1 kilo)

2lb (1 kilo) fresh chestnuts
⅓ pint (165ml) frozen chicken stock
1 onion
2oz (50gm) butter

pinch of ground cinnamon
1 teaspoon sugar
salt
pepper

To make
Make a cut in the skin of each chestnut, put them into boiling water and simmer for about 15 minutes, or until the skins burst open. Drain the chestnuts and remove the skins. Put the peeled chestnuts into a pan with the chicken stock and cook them gently until they are tender. Drain them, reserving the stock, and blend them to a purée in an electric blender or by rubbing them through a hair sieve. Chop the onion. Mix the onion, butter, cinnamon, sugar, salt and pepper and enough of the reserved stock into the chestnut purée to make a soft dough.

To freeze
While the Chestnut Stuffing is still slightly warm, pack it into a waxed carton. Set it aside to cool quickly and thoroughly. Seal, label, date and freeze.

To finish
Take the stuffing from the freezer the day before you need it and allow it to thaw out in the refrigerator. Use it to stuff the turkey at the neck end.

To serve
Slice the cooked stuffing along with the turkey. Although this stuffing is traditional at Christmas time, there is no reason why it should not be used at any time of the year.

Lemon and Watercress Stuffing

Try this unusual stuffing. It is quickly made from ingredients in the freezer.

Makes about 6oz (150gm)

4oz (100gm) frozen brown breadcrumbs
1 tablespoon frozen grated lemon rind
1 bunch of watercress

1 teaspoon sugar
salt
pepper
1 egg yolk

To make

In a warm basin, mix together the breadcrumbs and lemon rind. Chop the watercress leaves finely and add them, together with the sugar, salt and pepper, to the crumbs and rind. Mix well together and bind with egg yolk.

To freeze

This section is not of any real relevance, although if you do want to freeze the stuffing, follow the freezing instructions given for chestnut stuffing.

To finish

Use this stuffing inside two rolled breasts of lamb or a boned and rolled half leg of veal.

To serve

Serve the stuffing sliced with the meat.

Bread Sauce

Roast chicken and turkey simply must have Bread Sauce with them. This recipe is a very easy one.

Serves 8–10

1 pint (approximately $\frac{1}{2}$ litre) flavoured milk (see next recipe for béchamel sauce)
4oz (100gm) frozen white breadcrumbs

$\frac{1}{2}$oz (12gm) butter
salt
pepper
1 teaspoon crumbled frozen parsley
2 tablespoons cream

To make

To the warm, strained, flavoured milk, add all the remaining ingredients and mix the sauce well.

To freeze

Pour the Bread Sauce into empty yogurt cartons, cover and set aside to cool quickly and thoroughly. Seal, label, date and freeze.

To finish

Take the required quantity of sauce from the freezer and allow it to thaw out a little. Turn it into the top of a double boiler and heat it gently. Thin it down with a little milk or cream if necessary.

To serve

Serve the Bread Sauce hot with roast chicken, turkey and game.

Béchamel Sauce

This is a richer and tastier version of a basic white sauce and is also extremely useful as a basis of many different sauces.

Serves 8–10

1 pint (approximately ½ litre) milk
2 onions
1 blade of mace
6 peppercorns
1 small carrot

1oz (25gm) butter
1oz (25gm) flour
salt
pepper
cream

To make
Put the milk in a saucepan with the peeled and quartered onions, mace, peppercorns and chopped carrot. Bring slowly to the boil then let it sit for 15 minutes. Strain the milk. Melt the butter in a saucepan and beat in the flour. Remove the pan from the heat and gradually beat in the flavoured milk. Return the pan to the heat and cook the sauce until it thickens. Season it with salt and pepper.

To freeze
Pour the sauce into empty yogurt cartons, cover and set aside to cool quickly and thoroughly. Seal, label, date and freeze.

To finish
Take the required quantity of sauce from the freezer and allow it to thaw out a little. Turn it into a saucepan and heat it gently. Thin it down with cream if necessary.

To serve
Use the sauce as it is or add chopped, hard-boiled egg, cheese, crumbled frozen parsley, cucumber or almost anything of your choice to make a savoury dish.

Madeira Sauce

Here is a rich, savoury, wine sauce that is excellent with beef dishes.

Serves 8–10

3 shallots
1oz (25gm) butter
1oz (25gm) flour
1 pint (approximately ½ litre)
  frozen beef stock

⅛ pint (63ml) frozen tomato purée
1 teaspoon mixed herbs
salt
pepper
1 sherry glass Madeira

To make
Chop the shallots finely and fry them very gently in the butter. Sprinkle in the flour and stir over gentle heat for 1 minute. Gradually beat in the stock, tomato purée and herbs. Simmer the sauce for a few minutes then season it with salt and pepper and stir in the Madeira.

To freeze
Pour the sauce into empty yogurt cartons, cover and set aside to cool quickly and thoroughly. Seal, label, date and freeze.

To finish
Take the required quantity of sauce out of the freezer and allow it to thaw out a little. Turn it into a saucepan and heat it gently.

To serve
Serve the sauce hot with Beef Wellington (see page 82) or a home-boiled tongue.

Cherry Sauce

Sweet or savoury – this sauce goes with meat, poultry, game, fish or desserts. How useful to have such a versatile sauce in the freezer.

Serves 8–10

1lb (½ kilo) dark Morello cherries
½ pint (250ml) water
6oz (150gm) sugar

½oz (12gm) cornflour
¼ teaspoon ground cinnamon

To make

Wash and stone the cherries and boil them in the water until they are very soft. Put the cherries and water in the electric blender or rub them through a hair sieve. Mix in the sugar, and the cornflour and cinnamon blended with a little water. Boil the sauce for 5 minutes, or until it thickens slightly.

To freeze

Pour the sauce into ice cube trays and put them in the freezer. When the cubes are frozen, take them out of the trays and put them in a polythene bag. Seal, label, date and return to the freezer.

To finish

Take the required quantity of sauce cubes out of the freezer and heat them slowly in a saucepan.

To serve

Serve the sauce in a sauceboat with almost any meat. It is particularly nice with chicken, duck, grilled sole or as a sweet sauce poured over fresh fruit, sponge puddings or chocolate ice cream.

Brandy Sauce

This sauce is quite delicious and, besides being a variation of the traditional sauce for Christmas pudding, goes well with vanilla ice cream.

Serves 12–16

1 pint (approximately ½ litre) water
4oz (100gm) soft brown sugar
1lb (½ kilo) marmalade

2 lemons
¼ pint (125ml) brandy

To make

Put the water, sugar, marmalade and grated lemon rind into a saucepan and simmer for 15 minutes. Strain the sauce and stir in the juice from the lemons and the brandy.

To freeze

Pour the sauce into ice cube trays and put them in the freezer. When the cubes are frozen, take them out of the trays and put them in a polythene bag. Seal, label, date and return to the freezer.

To finish

Take the required quantity of sauce cubes out of the freezer and heat them slowly in a saucepan.

To serve

Serve the sauce poured over Christmas pudding or a sponge pudding, or over ice cream with a few chopped nuts and a blob of whipped cream on top.

Chocolate Sauce

Rich and gloriously fattening – a real treat!

Serves 8–10	8oz (200gm) dark chocolate	1 large can evaporated milk
	8oz (200gm) caster sugar	1 egg
	1oz (25gm) butter	$\frac{1}{8}$ pint (63ml) Curacao

To make Melt the chocolate in the top of a double boiler. Add the sugar, butter and evaporated milk. Mix the sauce very well, then gradually beat in the egg and the Curaçao.

To freeze Pour the sauce into empty yogurt cartons, cover and set aside to cool quickly and thoroughly. Seal, label, date and freeze.

To finish Take the required quantity of sauce from the freezer and allow it to thaw out a little. Turn it into a double boiler and heat it very gently, stirring continuously. Do not allow it to boil.

To serve Pour the sauce over raspberry ripple ice cream, or over Cream Puffs (see page 66) to make that superb dessert called Profiteroles au Chocolat.

Teatime

Elegance and lace; croquet and cucumber sandwiches; shades of a bygone era; these are the pictures that the word teatime conjures up in my mind. I think this idea stems very largely from the fact that tea, in its true sense, is disappearing. It is disappearing because people do not have time these days to sit around drinking "dishes of tea" in the middle of the afternoon, nor does the modern housewife have time to do all the baking of fresh bread and scones and cakes that a truly old-fashioned tea demands. But now and again, for instance on a lovely warm day when everyone is lazing in the garden or, at the other extreme, on a really chilly one when family and friends are grouped around a blazing log fire, tea is a real treat. Fresh new bread, scones and jam and cream, delicious, rich chocolate cake . . .

That's the "grown-up" version. But what about high tea for the children or high tea for all the family on a Saturday evening? In Scotland, high tea consists of a main course, such as bacon and eggs, fish and chips, cold meat and salad or spaghetti, followed by lots of bread and butter, scones, cakes, buns and biscuits and tea or coffee. Enough to sink a battleship, you might think but in Lancashire it's even worse – or perhaps better is the word – for there you are presented with a dessert, such as jelly and cream, fruit and custard or a trifle, as well as all the rest.

But whether your particular preference is for the dainty elegance of afternoon tea or the real keep-out-the-cold teas from the North, everyone loves home-made bread and cakes. And what a help the freezer is, because baking lends itself particularly well to freezing. Make a batch of cakes or biscuits when you have time and are in the mood and freeze them. You can keep them for as long as six months and when you have let them thaw out ready to eat, they will taste as fresh as on the day you baked them.

White Bread

(Illustrated opposite)

There is nothing quite like home-made bread, so make a batch, par-cook the loaves and pop them in the freezer.

Makes 6 loaves

7lb (3½ kilo) flour
3oz (75gm) salt
2oz (50gm) fresh yeast

4 level teaspoons sugar
3½ pints (approximately 1¾ litres) water

To make

Sift the flour and salt into a warm basin. In another basin cream the yeast with the sugar. Warm the water to lukewarm and add most of it to the yeast. Make a well in the centre of the flour and pour the yeast mixture into it. Knead it with your hand to a smooth, elastic dough adding the remaining wafer if necessary. Put a clean teatowel over the basin and set it aside in a warm place for about 1 hour, or until the dough has risen to double its size. Turn it out on to a floured board and knead it well to reduce its size and knock out all the air holes in the dough. Divide the dough into six and shape each into a loaf shape. Put into six greased loaf tins, set aside again in a warm place for 20 minutes to rise. Meanwhile, preheat the oven to hot, 450 deg F or gas 8 (230 deg C). Bake the loaves in the oven for 10–15 minutes, or until they are set. Then lower the oven temperature to moderately hot, 400 deg F or gas 6 (200 deg C) and continue baking for 45 minutes, or until they are pale brown and par-cooked. Turn the loaves out of the tins on to a wire cooling tray to cool.

To freeze

When cold, pack each loaf in a separate polythene bag, seal, label, date and freeze.

To finish

Preheat the oven to hot, 450 deg F or gas 8 (230 deg C). Take the required number of loaves out of the freezer and put them back in loaf tins. Bake the loaves in the oven for 35 minutes. Turn them out on to a wire cooling tray to cool.

To serve

Slice and use the bread as you think fit.

Soda Scones

This is an old-fashioned scone that is not seen much these days. Try it for a change.

Makes 8

2lb (1 kilo) flour
4 level teaspoons salt
4 level teaspoons baking soda

4 level teaspoons cream of tartar
1 pint (approximately ½ litre) buttermilk

To make

Heat the girdle or the solid electric hotplate or a large, strong frying pan slowly. Sift all the dry ingredients into a basin. Make a well in the centre and pour in the buttermilk. Mix it to a smooth, elastic dough. Divide the dough in two. Turn out on to a floured board and roll each piece out to a round about ¼–½ inch thick. Divide each round into four and bake each piece on a fairly hot, greased girdle, hotplate or frying pan for 3–4 minutes on each side. Cool the soda scones between two layers of clean teatowel.

To freeze

When cold, pack scones in polythene bags. Seal, label, date and freeze.

To finish

Take the required quantity of scones out of the freezer and allow them to thaw out for about 2 hours at room temperature.

To serve

Serve them for tea with fresh butter and home-made blackberry jelly. These scones are also lovely fried with bacon for breakfast.

Spoil yourself with home-made white bread (above), Scotch pancakes and gingerbread (page 64), macaroon tarts (page 65), truffles (page 66), pink and white cake and crunchy shortbread (page 69) . . . and strawberries and cream.

Scotch Pancakes
(*Illustrated on page 63*)

These pancakes are delicious spread with lots of butter.

Makes 30–40	
2lb (1 kilo) flour	4oz (100gm) sugar
4 level teaspoons baking soda	4 eggs
4 level teaspoons cream of tartar	1½ pints (approximately ¾ litre)
2 level teaspoons salt	buttermilk

To make   Heat the girdle or the solid electric hotplate or a large, strong frying pan slowly. Sift all the dry ingredients together into a basin. Beat the eggs well and gradually beat them, together with the buttermilk, into the dry ingredients to make a thick, smooth batter. Grease the girdle, hotplate or frying pan, make sure it is hot, then drop dessert-spoonfuls of the batter on to it. Cook on one side for 1–2 minutes, turn and cook the other side. Cool the pancakes between two layers of clean teatowel.

To freeze   When the pancakes are cold pack them in convenient quantities in polythene bags. Seal, label, date and freeze.

To finish   Take the required quantity of pancakes from the freezer and allow them to thaw out for about 1 hour at room temperature.

To serve   Serve them for tea with lots of fresh butter or fried, with bacon, for breakfast.

Gingerbread
(*Illustrated on page 63*)

A lovely spicy gingerbread is a useful stand-by to keep in the freezer.

Makes 2	
1lb (½ kilo) flour	8oz (200gm) butter
2 teaspoons baking soda	8oz (200gm) syrup
2 teaspoons mixed spice	8oz (200gm) treacle
2 teaspoons ground ginger	2 eggs, beaten
1 teaspoon cinnamon	scant ½ pint (250ml) milk
8oz (200gm) soft brown sugar	

To make   Preheat the oven to very moderate, 325 deg F or gas 3 (170 deg C) and line two loaf tins with greased greaseproof paper. Sift the flour, baking soda, mixed spice, ginger and cinnamon into a basin. In a saucepan melt together the sugar, butter, syrup and treacle, then pour the mixture, together with the beaten eggs, into a well in the centre of the dry ingredients. Mix well and add enough milk to give a soft consistency. Divide the mixture between the two loaf tins and bake in the oven for 1¼–1½ hours. Allow the gingerbread to cool in the tins.

To freeze   When the gingerbreads are cold, wrap them in kitchen foil. Seal, label, date and freeze.

To finish   Take the gingerbread from the freezer and allow it to thaw out for about 4 hours at room temperature. Unwrap it.

To serve   Serve the gingerbread plain or spread with butter for tea or morning coffee.

Doughnuts

Surprise the children now and again by giving them doughnuts from the freezer.

Makes 20

8oz (200gm) flour
1 level teaspoon salt
1oz (25gm) fresh yeast
2oz (50gm) sugar
2oz (50gm) butter

2 eggs
½ pint (250ml) milk
deep fat for frying
caster sugar

To make

Sift the flour and salt into a warm basin. In another basin cream the yeast with a teaspoonful of the sugar. Rub the butter into the flour until the mixture resembles fine breadcrumbs, then add the rest of the sugar. Beat the eggs lightly, warm the milk to just over lukewarm then beat it into the eggs. Make a well in the centre of the flour and pour in the yeast mixture and the egg mixture. Using your hands, mix and beat the ingredients to a smooth, elastic dough. Cover the basin and set it aside in a warm place for about 1 hour, or until the dough doubles in size. Turn the dough out on to a floured board and knead it to get rid of some of the air bubbles. Roll it out to ½ inch thick, cut into 20 rounds and make a hole in the centre of each one. Put these on a warm, greased tray, cover them and set them aside in a warm place for about 10 minutes to expand. Heat the deep fat to faintly smoking and fry the doughnuts, a few at a time, for 6–7 minutes, or until golden. Drain them well on kitchen paper.

To freeze

When the doughnuts are cold, pack them in convenient quantities in polythene bags. Seal, label, date and freeze.

To finish

Take the required quantity of doughnuts out of the freezer and allow them to thaw out for about 2 hours at room temperature. Unwrap them and toss them in caster sugar.

To serve

Serve the doughnuts for tea or morning coffee.

Macaroon Tarts

(*Illustrated on page 63*)

Lots of fillings may be put in pastry cases but this is slightly different from the usual.

Makes 20–24

1 packet (13½oz or 337gm) frozen
   shortcrust pastry
4oz (100gm) red jam
4 egg whites

6oz (150gm) caster sugar
4oz (100gm) ground almonds
glacé cherries
angelica

To make

Take the pastry from the freezer and allow it to thaw out sufficiently to enable you to roll it. Preheat the oven to cool, 300 deg F or gas 2 (150 deg C). Roll the pastry out to about ¼ inch thick, cut into 20–24 rounds and press into patty tins. Put a small teaspoonful of jam in each pastry case. Beat the egg whites until they are very stiff, fold in the sugar and ground almonds and put a spoonful in each pastry case. Bake in the oven for about 1 hour, or until the pastry is cooked and the filling crisp and golden brown. Turn the tarts out on to a wire cooling tray to cool.

To freeze

When the tarts are cold, pack them in convenient quantities in polythene bags. Seal, label, date and freeze.

To finish

Take the required number of Macaroon Tarts from the freezer and allow them to thaw for 2 hours at room temperature. Unwrap them and decorate with glacé cherries and angelica.

To serve

Serve the Macaroon Tarts for tea.

Cream Puffs

This choux pastry freezes excellently and may be made into round puffs or éclairs.

Makes 24–30

½ pint (250ml) water
4oz (100gm) butter
6oz (150gm) flour
1 level teaspoon salt
4 level teaspoons sugar

4 eggs
2 pints (approximately 1 litre)
    frozen double cream
icing sugar

To make

Preheat the oven to moderately hot, 400 deg F or gas 6 (200 deg C). Put the water and butter in a saucepan and bring slowly to the boil so that the butter melts. Sift the flour and salt together, then add it, together with the sugar, to the pan. Beat the mixture until it is smooth. Allow it to cool a little, then gradually beat in the eggs. Continue beating until a smooth, elastic paste results. Put the paste into a piping bag with a plain ½-inch (1·2cm) nozzle and pipe the mixture out into 24–30 rounds on to a well-greased baking tray. Bake them in the oven for 25 minutes. Take them out, make a small hole in each to let the air escape, turn the oven off and return the puffs to the oven for 7 minutes to dry out. Put the puffs on a wire cooling tray to cool.

To freeze

When the puffs are cold, pack them in convenient quantities in polythene bags. Seal, label, date and freeze.

To finish

Take the required quantity of puffs out of the freezer and a proportionate quantity of double cream. Allow the puffs and the cream to thaw out for about 1 hour at room temperature. Beat the cream until it is stiff. Unwrap the puffs and fill each with beaten cream. Dust the tops with icing sugar.

To serve

Serve them piled on a plate for tea or in dishes with chocolate sauce (see page 61) poured over for a special dessert.

Truffles

(Illustrated on page 63)

According to the size you make them, truffles are excellent for tea or as petits fours at the end of a dinner party.

Makes 20–40

10oz (250gm) bitter chocolate
2 tablespoons milk
6oz (150gm) butter
4oz (100gm) icing sugar

4 egg yolks
3oz (75gm) cake crumbs
4oz (100gm) chopped almonds

To make

Melt the chocolate slowly in the milk. Add the butter, stir well until it melts, then let the mixture cool a little. Mix in the icing sugar and beat in the egg yolks and the cake crumbs. Leave the mixture overnight in the refrigerator. Next day, roll the mixture into 20 large balls or 40 small balls and put on a baking sheet lined with kitchen foil.

To freeze

Put the truffles, on the baking sheet, into the freezer and, when they are frozen, transfer them in convenient quantities to polythene bags. Seal, label, date and freeze.

To finish

Take the required number of truffles out of the freezer, put them out on to a tray and allow them to thaw out for about 2 hours at room temperature. Roll each truffle in chopped almonds and put them in paper cases.

To serve

Serve the large truffles at teatime and the small ones as petits fours with coffee after dinner.

Victoria Sandwich

Although this a a simple basic recipe, it is invaluable for its varied uses. The mixture may be baked in two sandwich tins to make one large cake or in paper cases to make small, individual cakes.

Makes 1 sandwich sponge or 12–15 small cakes	4oz (100gm) butter 4oz (100gm) caster sugar 4 eggs, beaten 8oz (200gm) flour	½ teaspoon salt 2 tablespoons jam or ½ pint (250ml) frozen double cream icing sugar

To make Preheat the oven to moderate, 350 deg F or gas 4 (180 deg C). Cream the butter and sugar together until light and fluffy. Gradually beat in the eggs, then, using a metal spoon, fold in the sifted flour and salt. Turn the mixture into two 7-inch (18cm) greased and floured sandwich tins or 12–15 paper cases set in patty tins. Bake the large sponges in the oven for 20 minutes or the small cakes for 10–15 minutes. Turn the cakes out on to a wire cooling tray to cool in a draught-free place.

To freeze When the sponges are cold, put them in polythene bags. Seal, label, date and freeze.

To finish Take the sponges and cream (if used) out of the freezer and allow them to thaw for about 3 hours at room temperature. Sandwich the two large sponges together with jam and dust the top with icing sugar. If you have made little cakes, slice the tops off, fill them with whipped cream and replace the tops. Dust with icing sugar.

To serve Serve either for tea or as a basis for a dessert.

Swiss Roll

Surprise and delight your friends by giving them a home-made Swiss Roll for tea.

Makes 2	6 eggs 6oz (150gm) caster sugar vanilla essence 6oz (150gm) flour 2 level teaspoons baking powder	1 pint (approximately ½ litre) frozen double cream raspberry jam icing sugar

To make Preheat the oven to hot, 450 deg F or gas 8 (230 deg C). Line two Swiss roll tins with greaseproof paper. Grease and flour the paper. In a basin over a pan of hot water, beat the eggs and sugar together until they are thick and creamy. Add a few drops of vanilla essence. Sift the flour and baking powder together and fold them carefully into the egg mixture. Divide the mixture between the two prepared tins. Bake in the oven for 5–6 minutes. Turn the sponges out on to a sheet of greaseproof paper. Quickly cut off the edges, put another sheet of greaseproof paper on top of the sponge and roll the sponge up with the paper inside, as if it were a filling. Put the rolls on a wire cooling tray to cool.

To freeze When cold, unroll each roll carefully and replace the inside greaseproof paper with a sheet of polythene. Put both rolls in a polythene bag, seal, label, date and freeze.

To finish Take the required number of rolls from the freezer and allow them to thaw out for about 2 hours at room temperature. Take the proportionate amount of cream from the freezer and allow it to thaw out almost completely. Whip it until it is stiff. Carefully unroll the sponge and remove the polythene, spread the inside gently and carefully with jam and then with whipped cream. Roll up again. Dust the top with icing sugar.

To serve Serve the Swiss Roll for tea, or slice it and use it as a basis for trifle or top it with fruit and meringue for a quick dessert. Give the roll a coat of butter icing and decorate it for an Easter or Christmas cake.

Madeira Cake

A plain Madeira is a most useful cake to keep handy in the freezer.

Makes 2

10oz (250gm) butter
10oz (250gm) sugar
8 eggs, beaten
1lb ($\frac{1}{2}$ kilo) flour

1 level teaspoon baking powder
1 lemon
few pieces crystallised citron peel

To make

Preheat the oven to moderate, 350 deg F or gas 4 (180 deg C). Grease and line two loaf tins. Cream the butter and sugar together until light and fluffy. Gradually beat in the eggs, then, using a metal spoon, fold in the sifted flour and baking powder. Grate the rind of the lemon and mix it into the cake mixture. Divide the mixture between the two prepared tins and bake them in the oven for 1$\frac{1}{2}$–2 hours. Halfway through the cooking time, put strips of crystallised citron peel on top of each cake. Let the cakes shrink a little in the tins and then turn them out on to a wire cooling tray to cool.

To freeze

When the cakes are cold, wrap each in kitchen foil. Seal, label, date and freeze.

To finish

Take the required number of cakes from the freezer and allow them to thaw out for 4 hours at room temperature.

To serve

Serve the cake sliced for tea. This cake will keep well in a tin for a few days. Any stale scraps can be crumbled and re-frozen for later use in making truffles (see page 66).

Chocolate Cake

This cake may be completely finished before freezing, although I prefer to fill and ice it when I need it. That way the cake can also be used as a basis for desserts.

Makes 2

8oz (200gm) self-raising flour
$\frac{1}{2}$ level teaspoon baking powder
4oz (100gm) dark chocolate, grated
6oz (150gm) butter
6oz (150gm) caster sugar
4 eggs, beaten

Icing for 2 cakes:
2oz (50gm) dark chocolate
2oz (50gm) butter
3 teaspoons water
8oz (200gm) icing sugar

Filling for 2 cakes:
$\frac{1}{2}$ pint (250ml) frozen double cream

To make

Preheat the oven to moderate to moderately hot, 375 deg F or gas 5 (190 deg C). Grease and flour two square cake tins. Sift the flour and baking powder together and mix with the grated chocolate. Cream the butter and sugar together until light and fluffy. Gradually beat in the eggs, then, using a metal spoon, fold in the flour, baking powder and grated chocolate. Divide the mixture between the two prepared tins and bake in the oven for 10 minutes. Reduce the oven temperature to moderate, 350 deg F or gas 4 (180 deg C) and bake for a further 25–30 minutes. Allow the cakes to cool slightly in the tins then turn them on to a wire cooling tray.

To freeze

When the cakes are cold, wrap each in kitchen foil. Seal, label, date and freeze.

To finish

Take the required number of cakes from the freezer and allow them to thaw out for 4 hours at room temperature. For each cake take $\frac{1}{4}$ pint (125ml) frozen double cream from the freezer and allow it to thaw out almost completely. Whip the cream until stiff, split the cake and spread the middle with cream. Sandwich the two halves together. For the icing for each cake, heat half quantities of the chocolate, butter and water in a pan and beat in half the sugar. Beat until a smooth icing forms. When it is almost cold, spread it on top of the cake and decorate.

To serve

Serve the cake for tea. The decoration can be adapted for special occasions or pile apple and meringue on top of the chocolate sponge for a particularly delicious dessert.

Pink and White Cake

(Illustrated on page 63)

The children will love this attractive cake.

Makes 2

8oz (200gm) butter	Icing for 2 cakes:
8oz (200gm) sugar	1½lb (¾ kilo) butter
6 eggs, beaten	1½lb (¾ kilo) icing sugar
12oz (300gm) flour	2 teaspoons boiling water
2 teaspoons baking powder	cochineal
cochineal	crystallised violets

To make Preheat the oven to moderate to moderately hot, 375 deg F or gas 5 (190 deg C). Grease and flour four sponge sandwich tins. Cream the butter and sugar together until light and fluffy. Gradually beat in the eggs, then, using a metal spoon, fold in the sifted flour and baking powder. Put half the mixture into another basin and colour it pink with a few drops of cochineal. Then roughly fold the pink and white mixtures together again. Divide the mixture between the four tins and bake them in the oven for 20–25 minutes. Allow the cakes to shrink slightly in the tins, then turn them out on to a wire cooling tray to cool.

To freeze When the cakes are cold, wrap them in pairs in kitchen foil with a piece of foil between the two cakes. Seal, label, date and freeze.

To finish Take a pair of cakes from the freezer and allow them to thaw out for 3 hours at room temperature. To make the icing for each pair of cakes cream half the butter and work in half the icing sugar. Add a teaspoon of boiling water and blend it together well. Put half of it in another basin and colour it with cochineal. Sandwich the two cakes together with some of the icing and use the rest to cover it and decorate the top. Add crystallised violets for a finishing touch.

To serve Serve the cake for tea.

Crunchy Shortbread

(Illustrated on page 63)

Lovely, fresh shortbread biscuits with hardly any effort – make them, freeze them and bake them when needed.

Makes 40

12oz (300gm) butter	1 teaspoon salt
8oz (200gm) soft brown sugar	demerara sugar
1lb (½ kilo) flour	

To make Cream the butter and sugar together until light and fluffy, then work in the flour and salt. Knead the dough well, shape it into a 20-inch roll and cut into 40 ½-inch slices.

To freeze Put the slices back together in tens with a small piece of kitchen foil between each slice. Wrap each roll carefully in kitchen foil. Seal, label, date and freeze.

To finish Preheat the oven to moderate to moderately hot, 375 deg F or gas 5 (190 deg C). Take the required number of shortbread slices from the freezer and lay them out on a lightly greased baking sheet. Bake for 10 minutes, then take them out of the oven and sprinkle the tops with demerara sugar. Press the sugar in slightly. Return the shortbreads to the oven and bake for a further 10–15 minutes. Turn them on to a wire cooling tray to cool.

To serve Serve these lovely, fresh Crunchy Shortbread biscuits for tea or morning coffee.

single servings

How often have you said: "I love steamed pudding but I never have it at home. It simply isn't worth making for one"? And I would agree whole-heartedly. The same goes for stews, home-made soups, roast joints – after all, who wants to eat the same stew, soup or cold meat every night for a week? Of course, it would be a much more economical way of feeding yourself, but imagine the boredom of it!

Perhaps I should qualify my statement and say that there once was a time when I would have agreed whole-heartedly. Not any more. With a freezer the dilemma simply doesn't exist. You can make anything that takes your fancy and requires long, slow cooking, in the sure knowledge that you need be neither bored nor wasteful. Cook the dish in a quantity for four or six servings, have one portion immediately it is cooked and freeze the rest to eat later. If you live alone, this method will take a little planning and thought in the initial stages but it will soon become a way of life. It will also save you endless time and money and make for a much more varied diet.

Minestrone Soup
(Illustrated opposite)

This soup is a favourite, particularly when it is home-made. It usually takes a bit of time so it is worth making a quantity and freezing it.

Makes 4–6 servings

2 pints (approximately 1 litre) water	1 glass red wine
3oz (75gm) haricot beans	1lb (½ kilo) frozen diced mixed vegetables
1 large onion	4oz (100gm) cabbage, shredded
1 garlic clove	2oz (50gm) thin macaroni
1oz (25gm) lean bacon rashers	salt
2 tablespoons olive oil	pepper
1 teaspoon thyme	grated cheese
2 teaspoons oregano	
3oz (75gm) frozen tomato purée	

To make Heat ½ pint (250ml) of the water to boiling point and pour it over the beans. Leave them to soak for 1–2 hours. Peel and slice the onion, crush the garlic and chop the bacon. Heat the oil in a pan and fry the onion gently until it is soft. Add the garlic, bacon, herbs, tomato purée and wine. Bring the mixture to the boil and boil it rapidly for 5 minutes. Pour in the remaining water, the beans in their soaking water, bring the soup to the boil again and simmer it for 2 hours. Add the mixed vegetables, cabbage and macaroni to the pan and simmer for a further 20 minutes. Season the soup lightly. Help yourself to one serving and sprinkle grated cheese on top.

To freeze Turn the rest of the soup into a basin, cover and set it aside to cool quickly and thoroughly. Pour it into single-size waxed cartons, seal, label, date and freeze.

To finish Take the required quantity of soup from the freezer, turn it into a saucepan and gently heat it up.

To serve Serve the soup piping hot with grated cheese sprinkled on top.

Food for one need not be boring or time-consuming any more. Sit down to a meal of minestrone soup (above) and veal olives (page 75) followed by cheese and biscuits.

Kidney Soup

Like most home-made soups, kidney is well worth the effort of making.

Makes 4–6 servings	
1lb (½ kilo) frozen ox kidney	2 cloves
1 large onion	bouquet garni
1oz (25gm) butter	1oz (25gm) flour
½ teaspoon sugar	salt
2 pints (approximately 1 litre) water	pepper
	frozen parsley
8oz (200gm) frozen stew pack vegetables	fried croûtons

To make Take the kidney from the freezer and allow it to thaw out. Keep the juices that run out of the meat on thawing. Trim and cut up the kidney. Chop the onion and fry it in the butter until it is crisp and very well browned. Turn the heat down and add the kidney and the sugar. Fry the meat lightly. Add the kidney juices and the water. Bring the soup to the boil, add the vegetables, cloves and bouquet garni and simmer the soup for 2 hours. Strain the soup and thicken it with the flour blended with a little water. Chop some of the kidney and return it to the soup for garnish. Discard the rest. Help yourself to a serving. Sprinkle parsley on top and accompany with croûtons.

To freeze Turn the rest of the soup into a basin, cover and set it aside to cool quickly and thoroughly. Pour it into single-size waxed cartons, seal, label, date and freeze.

To finish Take the required quantity of soup from the freezer, turn it into a saucepan and gently heat it up.

To serve Serve the soup piping hot with crumbled frozen parsley sprinkled on top and with fried croûtons.

Creamed Tomato Soup

The addition of a little egg to this very quick soup at the finishing stage makes it extra nourishing.

Makes 4–6 servings	
2 pints (approximately 1 litre) frozen chicken stock	salt
	pepper
½ pint (250ml) frozen tomato purée	4–6 egg yolks
1oz (25gm) vermicelli	¼ pint (125ml) frozen single cream
2 teaspoons flour	

To make Take the stock and the tomato purée from the freezer and turn them into a saucepan. Heat them slowly. Add the vermicelli and cook for 15 minutes. Blend the flour with a little water and thicken the soup with it. Season to taste with salt and pepper. Put 1 egg yolk and a little cream in a soup bowl. Pour in one serving of hot but not boiling soup for a nourishing lunch or supper dish.

To freeze Turn the rest of the soup into a basin, cover and set it aside to cool quickly and thoroughly. Pour it into single-size waxed cartons, seal, label, date and freeze.

To finish Take the required quantity of soup from the freezer, turn it into a saucepan and gently heat it up. Put one egg yolk and a little cream into each soup bowl and pour the hot soup over.

To serve Serve the soup hot with crusty bread.

Cod Roe with Parsley Sauce

A quickly and easily made tasty supper dish.

Makes 4–6 servings

1 cod roe
1 pint (approximately ½ litre) frozen béchamel sauce (see page 59)

frozen parsley

To make

Bring some lightly salted water to the boil. Wash the cod roe, tie it in a piece of muslin and put it into the boiling, salted water. Boil it for 30–40 minutes, depending on size. Meanwhile, take the frozen béchamel sauce from the freezer. Heat it up gently in a pan and crumble in frozen parsley. Drain the roe, cut it in slices and skin the slices. Put one portion of roe on a plate and cover it with some of the parsley sauce for a delicious supper.

To freeze

Divide the remaining slices of roe between single-size foil dishes and pour sauce over each portion. Cover, seal, label, date and freeze.

To finish

Preheat the oven to moderate to moderately hot, 375 deg F or gas 5 (190 deg C). Take the required number of dishes of cod roe out of the freezer and place them on a baking sheet. Put them into the oven for 35 minutes to heat through thoroughly. Uncover the dishes and place them on serving plates.

To serve

Serve this delicious fish dish with creamed potatoes and buttered broad beans.

Pink Lamb Pie

Treat yourself to a lovely, juicy leg of lamb at the weekend and use the leftovers to make this superb pie.

Makes 4 servings

1lb (½ kilo) frozen carrots
12oz (300gm) swedes
8oz (200gm) onions
1½lb (¾ kilo) cold, cooked lamb
1oz (25gm) butter
salt
pepper

½oz (12gm) flour
½ pint (250ml) frozen lamb or beef stock
1 packet (4oz or 100gm) instant potato powder
2oz (50gm) butter
parsley sprigs

To make

Take the carrots from the freezer. Peel the swedes and onions and mince them together with the lamb. Melt the butter in a saucepan and fry the minced meat and vegetables in it. Season the mixture and stir in the flour. Pour in the stock and bring to the boil, stirring continuously. Divide the mixture between four single-size foil dishes. Meanwhile, make up the potato according to the instructions on the packet, then put the carrots through the grater attachment to the mincer and mix them into the potato. Spread this pink potato on top of each dish of lamb, fork it up and dot the top of each with butter. Put one dish under a medium grill to slightly brown and crisp the top. Garnish with a sprig of parsley and eat at once.

To freeze

Cover the remaining dishes with foil and set them aside to cool quickly and thoroughly. Seal, label, date and freeze.

To finish

Preheat the oven to moderately hot, 400 deg F or gas 6 (200 deg C). Take the required number of dishes of lamb pie out of the freezer and place them on a baking sheet. Put them into the oven for 25 minutes to heat through thoroughly. Remove the cover, turn the oven temperature up to hot, 425 deg F or gas 7 (220 deg C) and bake the pie for a further 10 minutes to crisp and brown the top. Garnish with a sprig of parsley.

To serve

Serve the dish by itself or with mango chutney and a tomato and cucumber salad.

Coq au Vin

If you feel like giving yourself a treat, try this dish. What you do not eat will freeze very well and be on hand for the next time you need cheering up.

Makes 6 servings

6 frozen chicken joints	1 dessertspoon mixed herbs
3oz (75gm) butter	salt
2 large onions	pepper
4oz (100gm) frozen sliced mushrooms	$\frac{1}{8}$ pint (63ml) brandy
1 bottle dry red wine	frozen parsley

To make — Take the chicken joints from the freezer and allow them to thaw out. Melt the butter in a large, strong saucepan or flameproof casserole. Chop the onions and fry them in the butter until they are well browned. Add the frozen mushrooms and fry them until they are quite soft. Add the chicken joints to the pan or casserole and fry them until the skins are crisp and golden. Pour in the wine and add the herbs and salt and pepper, making sure to scrape up any onion which may have stuck to the bottom of the pan. Cover the pan and simmer over a low heat for $1\frac{1}{2}$–2 hours. Pour in the brandy and put one portion on to a serving plate for you to eat at once. Crumble a little frozen parsley on top.

To freeze — Put a chicken joint into each of five single-size foil dishes and divide the gravy between them. Cover the dishes with foil and set them aside to cool quickly and thoroughly. Seal, label, date and freeze.

To finish — Preheat the oven to moderately hot, 400 deg F or gas 6 (200 deg C). Take the required number of dishes of chicken out of the freezer and place on a baking sheet. Put them into the oven for 35 minutes to heat through thoroughly. Turn out on to a plate and crumble frozen parsley on top.

To serve — This is a good special stand-by should an unexpected guest arrive. Serve it with buttered new potatoes and a green salad.

Smoked Trout

Simplicity itself – yet something special.

Makes 1 serving

1 frozen smoked trout	$\frac{1}{2}$ lemon
1 tablespoon horseradish sauce	parsley sprig
1 tablespoon double cream	

To make — Take the fish from the freezer the night before you need it and let it thaw out slowly in the refrigerator. Turn the horseradish sauce into a cup and mix in the cream.

To freeze — As the main ingredient comes from the freezer ready cooked, this section is not relevant.

To finish — When you are ready to serve the fish, put it on a plate. Using scissors, ease the skin from the belly of the fish and cut though the skin just below the head and just above the tail from the belly to the backbone. Ease the skin off the flesh and carefully roll it back, rather like a flap, to expose the flesh of the fish. Secure the roll of skin along the backbone with two halves of cocktail sticks. Garnish along the back with small lemon wedges or butterflies.

To serve — Put a good spoonful of horseradish cream on the plate and a sprig of parsley. Serve with a mixed salad.

Bacon and Chicken Crumble

Make a very quick meal for one using leftovers and ingredients from your freezer.

Makes 1 serving

¼ pint (125ml) frozen béchamel sauce (see page 59)
2oz (50gm) chopped, cooked chicken
2oz (50gm) chopped, boiled ham

2oz (50gm) frozen peas
½oz (12gm) frozen grated cheese
½oz (12gm) frozen white breadcrumbs
frozen parsley

To make

Take all the necessary ingredients from the freezer. Turn the béchamel sauce into a small saucepan and heat it very gently. Add the meats and continue heating for 5 minutes. Stir in the peas and turn the mixture into a greased pie dish. Mix the cheese and breadcrumbs together and sprinkle them on top of the mixture. Brown and crisp the top under a hot grill. Garnish with a parsley sprig.

To freeze

This is not really relevant in this case as the crumble is so quickly made. However, if you wish to freeze it, set the dish aside to cool quickly and thoroughly, then cover, seal, label, date and freeze.

To finish

If you have decided to freeze it again as above, preheat the oven to moderately hot, 400 deg F or gas 6 (200 deg C). Take the crumble from the freezer and place it on a baking sheet. Put it into the oven for 30 minutes to heat through thoroughly. Then remove the cover and crisp the top again under a hot grill.

To serve

Serve this meal-in-a-moment piping hot – no accompaniments are necessary.

Veal Olives
(Illustrated on page 71)

Traditionally this is made with beef but veal makes a nice change.

Makes 4 servings

4 frozen veal escalopes
2oz (50gm) frozen breadcrumbs
1oz (25gm) frozen chopped suet
2 teaspoons crumbled frozen parsley
½ teaspoon mixed herbs
1 teaspoon frozen grated lemon rind

salt
pepper
1 egg yolk
1oz (25gm) dripping
1 onion
¾ pint (375ml) frozen chicken stock
1oz (25gm) flour

To make

Take the veal from the freezer and allow it to thaw out for an hour or so. Keep the juices that run out of the meat on thawing. In a basin, mix together the crumbs, suet, parsley, herbs, lemon rind, salt and pepper and bind with egg yolk. Beat the veal well and cut each escalope in half. Put a little stuffing on each piece of meat, roll it up and tie with string. Melt the dripping in a saucepan. Chop the onion, then fry it gently in the dripping until it is transparent. Add the chicken stock, juices from the thawing meat and the veal olives. Simmer for 1 hour. Lift the veal olives out of the pan, remove the string and thicken the liquid with the flour blended with a little water. Pour the gravy over the veal olives and help yourself to a portion.

To freeze

Put two veal olives and some gravy into each of three single-size foil dishes, cover and set them aside to cool quickly and thoroughly. Seal, label, date and freeze.

To finish

Preheat the oven to moderate to moderately hot, 375 deg F or gas 5 (190 deg C). Take the required number of dishes of veal out of the freezer and place them on a baking sheet. Put them into the oven for 40 minutes to heat through thoroughly.

To serve

Serve the Veal Olives with duchess potatoes, peas and carrots.

Pork Crispies with Port Wine Sauce

Not worth having a roasting joint for one? Here is one of the many ways of making several tasty meals at one go from the leftovers.

Makes 4 servings

1lb (½ kilo) cold, cooked pork
4oz (100gm) flour
¼ teaspoon salt
1 egg

¼ pint (125ml) milk
deep fat for frying
½ pint (250ml) frozen port wine sauce (see page 89)

To make
Cut the pork into bite-sized chunks. Sift the flour into a basin with the salt, break in the egg and beat it into the flour using a wooden spoon. Gradually beat in the milk and continue beating until a thick, smooth batter results. Dip each piece of meat into the batter and fry them in faintly smoking, hot, deep fat until they are crisp and brown. Drain on kitchen paper and serve one portion hot with a little of the port wine sauce which has been gently thawed and heated up over a low heat.

To freeze
Lay the remaining, cooled Pork Crispies out on a tray and put them into the freezer. When they are frozen, pack them in single portion quantities in polythene bags. Seal, label, date and return to the freezer.

To finish
Take the Pork Crispies out of the freezer and, while they are still frozen, put them into faintly smoking, hot, deep fat to heat them through and regain their crispness. Take the required amount of port wine sauce from the freezer, turn it into a saucepan and heat it through gently.

To serve
Serve the Pork Crispies with the port wine sauce poured over and accompany with peas and carrots. Alternatively, serve the Pork Crispies on sticks as cocktail savouries.

Lemon Pancakes

Here again, it is hardly worth making up a pancake batter for one person but with the help of your freezer you can use the batter in the quantity you need and freeze the rest for use later.

Makes 4 servings

4oz (100gm) flour
¼ teaspoon salt
1 egg
1 tablespoon oil

½ pint (250ml) milk
1oz (25gm) butter
caster sugar
2 lemons

To make
Sift the flour and salt into a basin. Make a well in the centre and break the egg into it. Pour the oil over the egg. Using a wooden spoon, draw a little flour at a time into the egg and oil from the edges of the well until they are well blended together. Beat in the milk gradually. Beat the batter very well until little air bubbles show on the surface. Set it aside and let it settle for an hour or so. Put the butter into a knot of kitchen paper and use it to grease a hot pancake or omelette pan lightly. Pour a little batter into the pan to coat the surface thinly. Cook the pancake on one side for a minute or two, then toss it and cook the other side. Turn it out on to a sheet of greaseproof paper liberally sprinkled with sugar. Sprinkle the pancake with lemon juice and roll it up. Repeat this process with another pancake. This is your helping.

To freeze
This quantity of batter makes 8–10 pancakes altogether, so divide the remaining batter into three or four small yogurt pots. Seal, label, date and freeze.

To finish
Take the required quantity of batter out of the freezer and let it thaw out. It may need a little milk added to it if it has become too thick. Make the pancakes as described above.

To serve
Serve the pancakes hot and at least two to each helping with lots of lemon and sugar. Alternatively, pancakes are delicious with a savoury stuffing of, for instance, cooked chicken and a little béchamel sauce from the freezer mixed together. Or make this batter using only ¼ pint (125ml) milk for sweet or savoury fritters.

Gooseberry and Cinnamon Tart

How quick it is to make a gooseberry tart, even for one, with the help of the freezer.

Makes 4 servings

1 packet (13½oz or 337gm) frozen
  shortcrust pastry
8oz (200gm) frozen gooseberries
2 teaspoons cinnamon

sugar to taste
1 egg
caster sugar

To make

Take the pastry from the freezer and allow it to thaw out. Preheat the oven to moderately hot, 400 deg F or gas 6 (200 deg C). Roll the pastry out and cut it into four rounds. Line four single-size foil pie dishes with the pastry. Gather the pastry scraps together, roll them out again and cut four slightly smaller circles as lids for the tarts. Divide the gooseberries between the tarts and sprinkle each with cinnamon and sugar to taste. Top each with a pastry lid and seal the edges. Brush the top of one of the tarts with beaten egg and sprinkle it with caster sugar. Place it on a baking tray and bake in the oven for 5 minutes. Reduce the oven temperature to moderate to moderately hot, 375 deg F or gas 5 (190 deg C) and bake for a further 10–15 minutes. This one is yours.

To freeze

Wrap the remaining tarts individually in polythene bags, seal, label, date and freeze.

To finish

Preheat the oven to moderately hot, 400 deg F or gas 6 (200 deg C). Take the required number of tarts out of the freezer and remove the polythene bag. Brush the top of each tart with beaten egg and sprinkle with sugar. Bake in the oven for 35 minutes.

To serve

Serve the tart hot or cold with whipped cream or Cheddar cheese.

Marmalade Pudding

This is another of those glorious, old-fashioned recipes that is hardly worth making for one – unless you have a freezer.

Makes 4–6 servings

4oz (100gm) butter
4oz (100gm) sugar
2 eggs
5oz (125gm) flour

1 teaspoon baking powder
1 orange
boiling water
marmalade

To make

Cream the butter and sugar together until light and fluffy, then gradually beat in the eggs. Fold in the sifted flour and baking powder. Grate the orange and add the rind and a very little of the juice to the sponge mixture. Mix in 2 teaspoons boiling water. Put some marmalade in the bottom of a well greased, single-size (¼ pint or 125ml) pudding basin and spoon the sponge mixture on top. This one is for you when it is cooked. Divide the sponge mixture between the remaining three or five basins, omitting the marmalade. If you have no small basins, put all the sponge mixture into one well greased, large pudding basin, omitting the marmalade. Cover the basins with greased kitchen foil and steam the small puddings for 30 minutes or the large pudding for 1¼ hours. Turn out the one you have made to eat straight away on to a hot plate and let the melted marmalade pour over the top. Or, if you have made one big pudding, turn the pudding out on to a dish, cut a wedge for yourself and return the rest to the basin. Cover it again. Melt a little marmalade in a saucepan and pour it over your portion.

To freeze

Loosen the puddings in their basins, then leave them to cool still in their basins. Wrap each pudding in kitchen foil, seal, label, date and freeze. If you have made one pudding, divide it into portions. Wrap, seal, label, date and freeze each portion separately.

To finish

Take the required portions of Marmalade Pudding out of the freezer and steam them still in their wrappings for 40–45 minutes. Melt the proportionate amount of marmalade in a saucepan and pour over each serving.

To serve

Serve the Marmalade Pudding after a light main course.

Parties

Parties are to be enjoyed, a statement which may appear to be all too obvious. But I don't mean that they are to be enjoyed only by your guests. You too should enjoy your own party. After all, the conditions could not be better. You have decided to throw the party in the first place, to celebrate some sort of happy occasion; you have planned and looked forward to it; you have chosen what sort of party it will be; you have chosen the food and the guest list; you are on your home ground with people you know and presumably like, so what more do you need to get into a happy frame of mind?

However, there is the small question of the planning and preparation of the party. It need not be hard work. Indeed, it ought not to be. One of the first rules of party-giving is to plan carefully and well beforehand and then relax and enjoy yourself. Although your freezer can't exactly do the work for you, it can help enormously by allowing you to cook in a leisurely fashion well in advance of the event.

Obviously, there are dozens of different sorts of parties, ranging from the annual birthday and Christmas parties to a teenage pop party or a simple get-together for no particular reason. All require a different sort of approach as regards food and planning. On the following pages you will find a selection of ideas for different parties. Some are recipes that can be half or completely prepared and then frozen for later use; others are quickly prepared from basic frozen or a combination of frozen and fresh ingredients.

So, prepare, freeze, relax and enjoy!

Cucumber Crowns
(Illustrated opposite)

Make these pretty cocktail snacks quickly and easily from ingredients in the freezer.

Makes about 25

1 packet frozen prawn cocktail	melted butter
1 small packet frozen smoked salmon	1 large cucumber
	frozen parsley
5 large slices frozen bread	

To make Take the prawn cocktail and the smoked salmon from the freezer and allow them to thaw out for several hours in the refrigerator. Take the bread from the freezer and brush each slice on both sides with melted butter. Toast the bread on both sides and then cut each slice into five rounds using a fluted cutter. Slice the cucumber into ½-inch slices and cut away the middle of each (the middles can be added to a vegetable soup or a stew). Set each cucumber ring on a round of toast. Cut the smoked salmon into strips and fit a strip round the inside of each cucumber ring so that the ring of salmon stands up a little above the cucumber. Pile some prawn cocktail into the centre of each.

To freeze As you are using ingredients from the freezer and as cucumber does not freeze, this section is not relevant.

To finish Sprinkle each cucumber crown with crumbled frozen parsley.

To serve Place the Cucumber Crowns on a platter and serve them at a cocktail or buffet party.

Plan and prepare your party food well ahead, so that you can relax and enjoy yourself on the night. Serve your guests with cucumber crowns (above), cheese straws (page 80), mushroom vols-au-vent (page 81), chicken liver pâté (page 28), beef Wellington (page 82), turkey with apple stuffing and peppermint meringues (page 83), a fruit flan and, to drink, party punch (page 84) and lime cream soda (page 85).

Cheese Straws

(Illustrated on page 79)

An old and trusty favourite is this one. Everyone loves them and eats so many that it is useful to have a large quantity in the freezer.

Serves 10–20

1lb (½ kilo) flour
8oz (200gm) butter
8oz (200gm) lard
1½lb (¾ kilo) frozen grated cheese
salt
cayenne pepper

2 egg yolks
water to mix
1 egg white
frozen parsley
paprika pepper

To make

Preheat the oven to moderately hot, 400 deg F or gas 6 (200 deg C). Sift the flour into a basin. Rub in the butter and lard until the mixture resembles fine breadcrumbs, then mix in the grated cheese. Add salt and cayenne pepper to taste. Work in the egg yolks and a little water to make a firm pastry. Turn the cheese pastry out on to a lightly floured board and roll it out to ¼ inch thick. Cut the pastry into strips about 4 inches wide and keep the scraps on one side. Place the strips on the back of a baking tray and cut the pastry into fine, 4-inch long strips separating each one slightly to prevent them sticking together during cooking. Use the pastry scraps to make rings of cheese pastry. Bake the straws and rings in the oven for 3–5 minutes. Turn on to a wire cooling tray to cool.

To freeze

When the straws and rings are cold, pack them carefully into plastic boxes. Seal, label, date and freeze.

To finish

Take the required quantity of cheese straws and rings from the freezer just before you need them. Dip the ends of the straws in egg white and then alternately in crumbled frozen parsley and paprika pepper.

To serve

Arrange the straws attractively on a platter with some of them in bundles through the cheese rings and serve them with drinks.

Smoked Gems

These can be made well in advance, stored in the freezer and merely fried when needed.

Makes 50

6oz (150gm) butter
6oz (150gm) flour
1 pint (approximately ½ litre) milk
cayenne pepper
1lb (½ kilo) Brie cheese

6oz (150gm) frozen smoked haddock
 fillets
1 egg yolk
1 egg, beaten
breadcrumbs
deep fat for frying

To make

Melt the butter in a pan and stir in the flour. Cook gently for 1 minute. Remove the pan from the heat and gradually beat in the milk. Return the pan to the heat and cook the sauce until it thickens. Season with cayenne pepper, then set the sauce aside to cool. Meanwhile, take the rind off the cheese and rub the cheese through a sieve. Poach the smoked haddock fillets in a little water, drain them, flake finely and set aside to cool. When the white sauce is still just warm, beat in the egg yolk, cheese and fish. Put the mixture into the refrigerator to cool thoroughly and firm up enough for it to be rolled into marble-sized balls. Coat each in beaten egg and breadcrumbs.

To freeze

Place the Smoked Gems on a tray and put them into the freezer. When they are frozen, pack them in plastic boxes. Seal, label, date and return to the freezer.

To finish

Take the required quantity of Smoked Gems from the freezer and deep fry them for about 2 minutes, in faintly smoking, hot, deep fat. Drain on kitchen paper.

To serve

Serve the Smoked Gems hot on cocktail sticks.

Cheese and Pepper Whirls

These make a tasty nibble at a party for any age group.

Makes 40

8oz (200gm) back bacon rashers
2 small onions
2 large green peppers
8oz (200gm) Cheddar cheese
4oz (100gm) mayonnaise

2oz (50gm) tomato ketchup
1 small white loaf
melted butter
watercress

To make

Grill the bacon until it is crisp and chop it finely. Chop the onions and peppers finely. Grate the cheese, then mix the bacon, onions, peppers and cheese with the mayonnaise and tomato ketchup. Slice the loaf thinly into 20 slices and trim off the crusts. Spread the cheese mixture on to each slice, roll it up and cut in half.

To freeze

Place the whirls on a foil-lined baking tray and put them in the freezer. When they are frozen, pack them in convenient quantities in plastic boxes. Seal, label, date and return to the freezer.

To finish

Preheat the oven to moderately hot, 400 deg F or gas 6 (200 deg C). Take the required quantity of whirls out of the freezer and place them on a baking sheet. Brush them with melted butter and bake in the oven for 10–15 minutes, or until they are crisp and golden.

To serve

Serve on a dish paper on an attractive tray with a watercress garnish and with cocktail sticks.

Mushroom Vols-au-Vent

(Illustrated on page 79)

These may be made in various sizes with a variety of fillings to provide a substantial meal, a snack or a cocktail savoury.

Makes 9–12

1 packet (13½oz or 337gm) frozen
  puff pastry
1 egg yolk
¼ pint (125ml) frozen béchamel
  sauce (see page 59)

2oz (50gm) frozen sliced
  mushrooms
2 tablespoons frozen double cream
cucumber slices

To make

Take the pastry from the freezer and allow it to thaw out sufficiently to enable you to roll it. Preheat the oven to hot, 425 deg F or gas 7 (220 deg C). Roll the pastry out to a little less than ½ inch thick. Using a small, round cutter, cut out 9–12 circles, depending on size. Using a smaller round cutter mark a circle in the centre of each round. Put the pastry rounds on a wetted baking tray and brush the tops with beaten egg yolk to glaze. Bake them in the oven for about 15 minutes, or until risen and golden. Turn the vol-au-vent cases on to a wire cooling tray to cool.

To freeze

When the vol-au-vent cases are thoroughly cold, pack them in plastic boxes. Seal, label, date and freeze.

To finish

Preheat the oven to moderate, 350 deg F or gas 4 (180 deg C). Take the required number of vol-au-vent cases out of the freezer and the proportionate amount of béchamel sauce, mushrooms and cream. Put the vol-au-vent cases into the oven for about 30 minutes to heat through thoroughly. Meanwhile, turn the béchamel sauce into a small saucepan and add the mushrooms. Heat them gently, stirring constantly. Stir in the cream. Take the vol-au-vent cases from the oven and carefully remove the cut inner circle tops. Fill each case with a little mushroom mixture and replace the top. Decorate with a half slice of cucumber.

To serve

Serve hot or cold as a cocktail snack.

Beef Wellington

(Illustrated on page 79)

This is an expensive luxury dish and very impressive for a special party. It lends itself admirably to being prepared and frozen well before it is required.

Serves 8–12

1 packet (13½oz or 337gm) frozen
   puff pastry
salt
pepper
little brandy
1 whole fillet of beef, about 4–4½lb
   (2–2¼ kilo)

8 fat bacon rashers
12oz (300gm) chicken liver pâté (see
   page 28)
flour
1 egg yolk
1 pint (approximately ½ litre)
   Madeira sauce (see page 59)

To make   Take the pastry from the freezer and allow it to thaw out sufficiently to enable you to roll it. Preheat the oven to hot, 450 deg F or gas 8 (230 deg C). Rub the salt, pepper and the brandy well into the fillet of beef and put it on a rack in a roasting tin. Cover the top of the meat with the bacon rashers and put the meat into the oven for about 15 minutes, to seal in the juices. Throw the bacon away and set the beef aside to cool completely. Roll the pastry out to an oblong about three times the width of the meat and about half as long again as the fillet. Spread the chicken liver pâté over the top, sides and ends of the fillet and place it, upside down, on the pastry. Turn in the sides and the ends of the pastry to make a parcel of the meat and seal the edges with water. Turn the parcel over and decorate the top with leaves made out of the scraps of pastry.

To freeze   Sprinkle the beef parcel lightly with flour and wrap it carefully in a double layer of cling film. Seal, label, date and freeze.

To finish   Take the beef out of the freezer the evening before you need it and allow it to thaw out almost completely in the refrigerator. Next day, preheat the oven to hot, 425 deg F or gas 7 (220 deg C). Brush the top of the pastry with beaten egg yolk and place the beef on a baking sheet. Put it into the oven and cook for 40–45 minutes, or until the pastry is crisp and golden. Take the Madeira sauce out of the freezer and heat it gently in a saucepan.

To serve   Serve Beef Wellington hot with the Madeira sauce, boiled new potatoes, baked tomatoes and a fresh green salad. It may also be served cold, garnished with parsley and accompanied with a mixed salad.

Turkey with Apple Stuffing

(Illustrated on page 79)

For a change, why not have turkey in midsummer? It's so easy when you have a freezer.

Serves 15–20

6oz (150gm) rice
liver from the turkey
2 onions
6oz (150gm) frozen apple slices
4oz (100gm) chopped almonds
3 tablespoons crumbled frozen
  parsley

3oz (75gm) butter
2 teaspoons ground cinnamon
salt
pepper
1 egg yolk
1 frozen turkey, about 12lb (6 kilo)
bacon fat

To make

Cook the rice in boiling, salted water until it is almost tender. Drain, rinse and dry it. Cook the turkey liver in a little water, then drain and chop it finely. Chop the onions and apple slices finely, then mix them together with all the ingredients except the turkey and bacon fat.

To freeze

Put the stuffing into a polythene bag, seal, label, date and freeze.

To finish

Take the turkey from the freezer and allow it to thaw out for 36 hours at room temperature. The stuffing will need 4 hours to thaw out. Preheat the oven to moderate, 350 deg F or gas 4 (180 deg C). Pack the apple stuffing into the neck end of the turkey. Rub the turkey over with bacon fat and roast it in the oven for 3½ hours.

To serve

Serve the turkey hot garnished with grilled sausages and bacon rolls. Accompany it with roast potatoes, Brussels sprouts, gravy and bread sauce (see page 58). Alternatively, serve it cold garnished with watercress and accompanied with a fresh, mixed salad.

Peppermint Meringues

(Illustrated on page 79)

The colour of meringues can be varied merely by adding different food colourings, but these delicate pale green meringues with white cream look very pretty on a party table.

Serves 18–20

4 egg whites
8oz (200gm) caster sugar
4 drops peppermint essence

2–3 drops green food colouring
1 pint (approximately ½ litre) frozen
  double cream

To make

Preheat the oven to very cool, 225 deg F or gas ¼ (110 deg C). Put the egg whites into a basin and whisk them (preferably with a balloon whisk) until they are quite stiff. Quickly whisk in 2oz (50gm) of the caster sugar, the essence and colouring. Carefully fold in the remaining sugar. Pipe or spoon the meringue out into rounds on to a sheet of oiled and floured greaseproof paper on a baking tray. Bake in the oven for 3–4 hours, or until the meringues are dry. Transfer them to a wire cooling tray to cool.

To freeze

When the meringues are cold, pack them carefully into plastic boxes. Seal, label, date and freeze.

To finish

Take the required number of meringues and the proportionate amount of cream from the freezer 1 hour before they are required. Beat the cream until it is stiff, then use it to sandwich the meringue shells together in pairs.

To serve

Serve the meringues in paper cases for tea or a party or with thawed out frozen fruit as a dessert.

Barbados Sangaree

This rum punch is a wildly exotic drink with a real flavour of West Indian luxury. Make it and freeze it in cubes for use in as little or as large a quantity as you can stand!

Serves 6–8

1 bottle Barbados rum
1 Bramley's Seedling apple
cloves
6 cream cracker biscuits
1½ pints (approximately ¾ litre) water

freshly grated root ginger
sugar to taste
1 lemon
lemon rind
mint leaves

To make   Turn the rum into a wide-necked jar, stick the apple with lots of cloves and put the apple in the rum. Seal the jar and set it aside for a week or so. Put the cracker biscuits under the grill and toast them slowly on both sides until they are burnt. Put the burnt biscuits into the rum, add the water, a little root ginger, sugar to taste and the grated rind and juice of the lemon. Set the mixture aside for 30 minutes, then strain it.

To freeze   Pour the Sangaree into ice cube trays and put them in the freezer. When they are frozen, remove the iced cubes from the trays and pack them in convenient quantities in polythene bags. Spray a little soda water in each bag to prevent the cubes sticking together. Seal, label, date and return to the freezer.

To finish   Take the required number of cubes from the freezer, put them in glasses or a jug, cover with a cloth and allow them to thaw out at room temperature.

To serve   Decorate each glass with a twist of lemon rind and a mint sprig. Put two straws in each glass and serve well chilled as a cocktail on a warm evening.

Party Punch
(Illustrated on page 79)

As a fairly inexpensive drink but one with a kick to it, this punch is excellent for any party.

Serves 40

1 can frozen concentrated orange juice
1 can frozen concentrated grapefruit juice
1 can frozen concentrated pineapple juice
sugar to taste

8 small bottles ginger ale
2 bottles dry white wine
1 jar maraschino cherries
2 oranges
2 lemons
ice cubes

To make   Reconstitute the frozen fruit juices with half the recommended amount of water. Mix them together and add sugar to taste.

To freeze   Pour the mixed juices into ice cube trays and put them in the freezer. When they are frozen, remove the iced cubes from the trays and pack them in convenient quantities in polythene bags. Spray a little soda water in each bag to prevent the cubes sticking together. Seal, label, date and return to the freezer.

To finish   Put all the fruit juice cubes into a punch bowl, pour on the chilled ginger ale and white wine. Mix well. Drain and discard the juice from the cherries and slice the oranges and lemons. Add the fruit to the punch together with ice cubes, if liked.

To serve   Serve the punch in a large punch bowl and ladle it out into glasses.

Lime Cream Soda

(Illustrated on page 79)

A simple and attractive drink which the children will love.

Serves 1	**1 measure of lime juice cordial**	**1 bottle tonic water**
	2 scoops raspberry ripple ice cream	**1 sponge finger**

To make   Pour the lime juice cordial into a tall glass. Add the ice cream and pour the tonic water into the glass.

To freeze   The ice cream obviously comes from the freezer but otherwise this section is not relevant in this case.

To finish   Lay the sponge finger across the top of the glass.

To serve   Serve very cold on any occasion. The flavours of the ice cream and liquid may, of course, be varied. For example, try iced coffee with creamy vanilla ice cream or iced drinking chocolate with chocolate ice cream and topped with a peppermint meringue shell (see page 83). Plain lemonade combined with lemon sorbet and topped with a slice of lemon also makes a delicious drink.

Grand occasion dinners

No book is complete without some really super recipes for special occasions. So, as a climax to the recipe chapter of this Freezer Feast, I have chosen four dinner party menus which are well-balanced for colour, flavour and "weight". None of the meals is too heavy, no dish is too difficult or time-consuming to prepare but they all look "cordon bleu".

Not only does your freezer allow you time to prepare such sumptuous meals at a relaxed speed but think of the delight of serving a dinner of asparagus, salmon and strawberries at Christmas time in Britain!

Before meals such as these, I like to offer sherry, with a choice of sweet or dry, and perhaps another wine-based aperitif such as a Vermouth. I feel spirits detract from the full enjoyment of the flavour of a meal besides not mixing too well with wine served with dinner. You can, of course, provide a different wine for every course but, in general, one wine throughout a meal is quite sufficient.

For the first menu with salmon as a main course, I would suggest that you serve a champagne, or one of the popular-priced, sparkling white wines which can give the feeling of the opulence of champagne without making too much of a hole in the housekeeping allowance. With the pheasant, how about a rich, full-bodied claret brought to room temperature? There are a number of very palatable Spanish, claret-type wines on the market at under £1. With the pork try a French or Portuguese rosé, a German hock or even a British apple or gooseberry wine. The range is so wide that the choice is yours, but essentially I would suggest a light, medium dry wine, well chilled. And for the last menu? Have you ever tried a new beaujolais lightly chilled? It is delicious but is only available from the middle of November until the following Easter when it becomes Vin de l'Année and has not, to my mind, quite the excitement of the Beaujolais Nouveau. Otherwise a five- or six-year-old beaujolais would go equally well with the lamb chops.

Whether you provide brandy and liqueurs is up to you but one essential adjunct to a really good dinner is a bottomless pot of coffee.

Asparagus in Hollandaise

(*Illustrated opposite*)

A Hollandaise makes a delicious change from plain melted butter with the delicate flavour of asparagus.

Serves 6–8

2 packets frozen asparagus	**4 tablespoons water**
6oz (150gm) butter	**4 egg yolks**
salt	**salt**
6 tablespoons white vinegar	**pepper**

To make

Take the asparagus from the freezer and put it in a pan with 2oz (50gm) of the butter and a little salt. Cover the pan and cook the asparagus slowly for about 20 minutes. Meanwhile, put the vinegar into a saucepan and boil it rapidly until it is reduced to 2 tablespoonfuls. Add the water. Put the egg yolks in a basin and pour the vinegar and water over them. Melt 2oz (50gm) butter in a basin and whisk in the egg mixture. Put the basin in a pan of hot water and stir in the remaining butter. Season the sauce and keep it warm.

To freeze

As the asparagus has come from the freezer and as the sauce is so quick to make, this section is not relevant.

To finish

Drain the asparagus carefully and arrange the spears on a dish. Pour the sauce over. Alternatively, serve the asparagus in bundles on a folded napkin on a large platter. Hand the sauce separately in a sauceboat.

To serve

Serve the asparagus with the Hollandaise as a starter to a meal.

Dressed Salmon

(*Illustrated opposite*)

No need to confine your menus to the seasonal availability of food – have delicious Scotch salmon at any time of year.

Serves 8

6lb (3 kilo) frozen salmon	**$\frac{1}{4}$ pint (125ml) vinegar**
1 bouquet garni	**1 cucumber**
2 bayleaves	**mustard and cress**
salt	**2 lemons**

To make

Take the salmon from the freezer and allow it to thaw out for about 6 hours at room temperature. Half fill the fish kettle with water, add the bouquet garni, bayleaves, pinch of salt and the vinegar. Bring it to the boil. Carefully put the whole salmon into the water and over a medium heat bring the water back to the boil. Allow it to simmer for 5–10 minutes, then take the fish kettle off the heat and let the salmon cool completely in the water. Drain the fish and remove the skin.

To freeze

This section is not relevant as the fish has come from the freezer.

To finish

Lay the fish on a platter and decorate it with slices of cucumber, mustard and cress and slices of lemon.

To serve

Serve the salmon with fresh mayonnaise, new potatoes and salad. The leftovers may be made into a salmon loaf, a kedgeree or even sandwich filling (see page 52) and frozen for later use.

Delight your guests with a meal of asparagus in hollandaise and dressed salmon (above) and strawberry Pavlova (page 88) prepared from the freezer and served out of season.

Strawberry Pavlova
(*Illustrated on page 87*)

This looks absolutely gorgeous on any dinner table but imagine how much more impressive to serve such a dessert in midwinter!

Serves 8

6 egg whites
12oz (300gm) caster sugar
3 teaspoons cornflour
3 teaspoons white vinegar

1 pint (approximately ½ litre) frozen double cream
1½lb (¾ kilo) frozen strawberries

To make

Preheat the oven to very cool, 250 deg F or gas ½ (130 deg C). Beat the egg whites with 1 teaspoon of the sugar until they are very stiff. Beat in half the sugar. Fold in the remaining sugar, the cornflour and the vinegar. Spread the mixture out into four 8–10 inch rounds on oiled and floured greaseproof paper on baking trays and bake in the oven for 1 hour. Reduce the oven temperature to very cool, 225 deg F or gas ¼ (110 deg C) and bake for a further 30 minutes. Set them aside to cool.

To freeze

When the Pavlovas are cold, pack them in individual polythene bags in a box. Seal, label, date and freeze.

To finish

Take the four Pavlovas from the freezer and allow them to thaw out for about 1 hour at room temperature. Take the cream and the strawberries from the freezer at the same time. Let the strawberries thaw out spread on kitchen paper. Beat the cream until it is stiff and slice the strawberries. Sandwich the Pavlovas together with whipped cream and sliced strawberries and decorate the top similarly.

To serve

Serve on a silver dish or a pedestal cake plate. This makes an impressive dessert and can look equally attractive made with frozen peaches or frozen redcurrants.

Avocado Soup

The creamy delicacy of this soup is a real treat.

Serves 8

4 avocado pears
2oz (50gm) butter
salt
black pepper
1 tablespoon lemon juice
3 pints (approximately 1½ litres) frozen chicken stock

¼ pint (125ml) frozen single cream
1 bouquet garni
2 onions
frozen parsley

To make

Take the stones out of the avocados and remove the skin from the flesh. Mash the flesh with the softened butter, salt, pepper and lemon juice.

To freeze

Pack the avocado purée into waxed cartons and put a piece of polythene sheeting on top of the pulp to prevent discoloration. Seal, label, date and freeze.

To finish

Take the avocado purée, the chicken stock and the cream from the freezer and allow them to thaw out for about 2 hours at room temperature. Turn the chicken stock into a saucepan and add the bouquet garni and peeled and quartered onions. Bring it slowly to the boil and simmer for 30 minutes. Strain and reheat. Take the stock off the heat and carefully fold in the avocado purée.

To serve

Pour the soup immediately into soup bowls, stir in a little cream and sprinkle crumbled frozen parsley on top. Serve with thinly sliced brown bread.

Pheasant with Port Wine Sauce

Serve pheasant for a summer meal to surprise and delight your guests.

Serves 8

1 pint (approximately ½ litre)
  pheasant giblet stock
  (see method)
salt
pepper
8oz (200gm) butter
2oz (50gm) lean bacon, minced
1 onion
1oz (25gm) flour
1 bayleaf

1 teaspoon thyme
6 cloves
1 lemon
1 wine glass of port wine
1 tablespoon redcurrant jelly
2 brace pheasant
4oz (100gm) fat bacon rashers
frozen breadcrumbs
watercress
tail feathers

To make

Put the pheasant giblets into about 1½ pints (approximately ¾ litre) cold water with a little seasoning and bring them slowly to the boil. Simmer for 30 minutes then strain the giblet stock. Melt 2oz (50gm) of the butter and gently fry the minced bacon and finely chopped onion. Stir in ½oz (12gm) flour and cook it until lightly brown. Add 1 pint (approximately ½ litre) giblet stock, the bayleaf, thyme and cloves. Bring to the boil and simmer the sauce for 30 minutes. Strain it, add the juice of the lemon, season it to taste and stir in the port wine and redcurrant jelly. Set the sauce aside to cool.

To freeze

When the sauce is cold, pour it into conveniently sized waxed cartons. Seal, label, date and freeze. Make sure that the pheasant have been properly hung as they will not mature any more during or after freezing. Wrap each pheasant closely and carefully in freezer foil. Seal, label, date and freeze.

To finish

Take the pheasant from the freezer a couple of hours before you require to start cooking them and allow them to thaw at room temperature. Any juices from the pheasant can be added to the sauce. Preheat the oven to moderate, 350 deg F or gas 4 (180 deg C). Take the sauce from the freezer. Cover each pheasant with bacon rashers and wrap each in kitchen foil. Place in a roasting tin and roast in the oven for about 30 minutes. Remove the foil and the bacon, baste the pheasant with 4oz (100gm) melted butter and sprinkle with the remaining ½oz (12gm) flour. Increase the oven temperature to moderately hot, 400 deg F or gas 6 (200 deg C) and return the pheasant to the oven for 5 minutes. Put the sauce into a saucepan and heat it through gently. Melt the remaining 2oz (50gm) butter and fry the frozen breadcrumbs until they are golden.

To serve

Put the pheasant on to a large platter and garnish with browned crumbs, watercress and tail feathers. Pour the sauce into a sauceboat. Accompany with new potatoes, leaf spinach and baked tomatoes.

Cream Cheese Layer

Half of this dessert can be made well in advance and then it needs only to be assembled on the day.

Serves 8–10

½ pint (250ml) pancake batter
(see lemon pancakes, page 76)
1 pint (approximately ½ litre) frozen
double cream

1lb (½ kilo) mild soft cream cheese
4oz (100gm) icing sugar

To make

Make nine thin pancakes out of the batter. Leave them to cool layered between sheets of greaseproof paper and between two plates.

To freeze

When the pancakes are cold, put a layer of polythene film between each pancake and put them in a polythene bag. Seal, label, date and freeze.

To finish

Take the pancakes and the double cream from the freezer and allow them to thaw out for 2 hours at room temperature. Spread four of the pancakes liberally with cream cheese and sprinkle each with sifted icing sugar. Whip the cream and spread another four pancakes with cream. Layer the cheese and cream pancakes alternately and top with the remaining pancake. Sprinkle the top with icing sugar through a cut-out paper shape to form a pattern.

To serve

Serve the Cream Cheese Layer as a dessert alone or with frozen blackberries. Cut it down in wedges like a cake.

Jellied Consommé

This makes an elegant and delicious starter to a meal.

Serves 8–10

3lb (1½ kilo) beef bones
1 pig's trotter
4 sticks celery
2 onions
cloves
1 carrot
1 bouquet garni
salt

peppercorns
3 pints (approximately 1½ litres)
water
¼ pint (125ml) sherry
4–5 slices bread
ice cubes
frozen parsley

To make

Put all the ingredients except the sherry, slices of bread, ice cubes and parsley into a large saucepan and bring to the boil. Strain off the scum that forms. Half cover the pan and simmer the soup for 3 hours. Strain the liquid through muslin into a large basin. Cover it and set it aside to cool. When it is cold take the fat off the top. Add the sherry.

To freeze

Turn the jellied consommé into conveniently sized waxed cartons. Seal, label, date and freeze.

To finish

Take the consommé from the freezer and allow it to thaw out for 3 hours at room temperature. Turn it out into a basin and chop it up. Toast the bread slices and remove the crusts.

To serve

Pile the chopped consommé into small dishes. Place these dishes on ice cubes in soup bowls and sprinkle the consommé with crumbled frozen parsley. Serve with fingers of fresh toast.

Gooseberry Stuffed Pork

Gooseberries make a tasty stuffing for pork.

Serves 6–8

4–5lb (2–2½ kilo) frozen boned and rolled loin of pork
1lb (½ kilo) frozen gooseberries
4oz (100gm) frozen wholemeal breadcrumbs

1 tablespoon chopped mint
2 tablespoons soft brown sugar
1 egg
salt
2 teaspoons arrowroot

To make

Take the pork from the freezer and allow it to thaw out for 24 hours in the refrigerator. Take the gooseberries from the freezer and allow them to thaw out. Preheat the oven to moderate, 350 deg F or gas 4 (180 deg C). Cut up half the gooseberries and mix them with the breadcrumbs, mint and half the sugar. Bind with the egg. Untie the meat and lay it out flat. Spread the inside with the stuffing and roll the meat up again. Re-tie. Rub the skin with salt and roast it in the oven for about 2½ hours. Put the remaining gooseberries into a pan with the remaining sugar and a little water. Stew them until tender, strain them and thicken with the arrowroot blended with a little water.

To freeze

As you are using frozen ingredients, this section is hardly relevant. However, the gooseberry sauce freezes well. Pour it into waxed cartons, seal, label, date and freeze.

To finish

If you have frozen the sauce, take it from the freezer and reheat it gently.

To serve

Place the roast pork on a platter and pour the sauce into a sauceboat. Accompany with roast potatoes and spring greens.

Raspberry Slice

There's a Continental flavour about this most attractive dessert.

Serves 8–10

1 packet (13½oz or 337gm) frozen puff pastry
1 egg yolk
1 packet (1lb or ½ kilo) marzipan
1lb (½ kilo) frozen raspberries

½ pint (250ml) frozen double cream
¼ pint (125ml) water
4oz (100gm) caster sugar
cochineal
3 teaspoons arrowroot

To make

Take the pastry from the freezer and allow it to thaw out sufficiently to enable you to roll it. Preheat the oven to hot, 425 deg F or gas 7 (220 deg C). Roll the pastry out to a rectangle about 14 inches by 8 inches. Work about half the egg yolk into the marzipan, divide it in two and roll each piece out to a sausage 14 inches long. Place a roll of marzipan on the pastry along each of the long sides and fold the edges of the pastry over to enclose the marzipan. Seal the edges with water. Brush the "walls" of pastry with the remaining egg yolk and make a few slits with a sharp knife along the "walls". Put the pastry on to a wetted baking tray and bake it in the oven for 15–20 minutes, or until the pastry is crisp and golden. Turn the pastry on to a wire cooling tray to cool.

To freeze

The pastry may be frozen at this stage, though I prefer to make it as I need it. However, if you want to freeze it, put it into a polythene bag, seal, label, date and freeze.

To finish

Take the raspberries from the freezer and allow them to thaw out spread on kitchen paper. If you have frozen the pastry, take it from the freezer and allow it to thaw out, together with the cream. Boil together the water, sugar and a few drops of cochineal and thicken the syrup with arrowroot blended with a little water. Set it aside to cool. Whip the cream until it is stiff. Remove and discard the middle of the pastry slice leaving a thin base. Spread half the cream on the base of the pastry and top with almost all the raspberries. Carefully pour over the thickened syrup and put the slice in the refrigerator to set. Pipe the rest of the cream on top and decorate with a few whole raspberries.

To serve

Serve this delicious dessert cut in slices.

Iced Madras Cocktail

A curry cocktail makes a change from fruit juices as an easy appetizer.

Serves 8

4 spring onions
1oz (25gm) butter
1 tablespoon hot curry powder
1oz (25gm) flour
2 pints (approximately 1 litre) frozen chicken stock
bouquet garni
1 tablespoon frozen grated lemon rind

2 tablespoons crumbled frozen parsley
⅛ pint (63ml) frozen tomato purée
2 teaspoons arrowroot
ice cubes
toasted almonds

To make   Chop the onions finely and fry them gently in butter. Add the curry powder and cook gently for 1 minute. Stir in the flour, then pour in the stock, stirring continuously. Add all the other ingredients except the arrowroot, ice cubes and almonds. Simmer for 20 minutes. Strain the cocktail and thicken it slightly with the arrowroot blended with a little water. Set aside to cool.

To freeze   When the cocktail is cold pour it into ice cube trays and put them in the freezer. When they are frozen, remove the iced cubes from the trays and pack them in convenient quantities in polythene bags. Spray a little soda water in each bag to prevent the cubes sticking together. Seal, label, date and return to the freezer.

To finish   Take the cubes from the freezer, put them in a basin and allow them to thaw out at room temperature. When the cocktail is thawed, stir it well and pour it into attractive glasses.

To serve   Put a couple of ice cubes in each glass and top the Curry Cocktail with a sprinkling of chopped toasted almonds. Serve it well chilled.

Lamb Cutlets in Pastry

Use ingredients from the freezer, half prepare the cutlets, freeze them and finish the dish with a minimum of fuss.

Serves 8

2 packets (13½oz or 337gm) frozen puff pastry
16 frozen lamb cutlets
salt
pepper
garlic salt

1 pint (approximately ½ litre) frozen béchamel sauce (see page 59)
deep fat for frying
3 hard-boiled eggs
½ cucumber

To make   Take the pastry and the cutlets from the freezer and allow them to thaw out for 1 hour at room temperature. Season the cutlets with salt, pepper and garlic salt and put them under a hot grill to brown and seal them and to cook them partially. Drain the cutlets well on kitchen paper, leave to cool, then put them in the refrigerator to chill thoroughly. Meanwhile, roll the pastry out very thinly and cut it into 16 pieces large enough to wrap the meaty heads of the cutlets. Place each cutlet on a piece of pastry and completely enclose the meat with it. Seal the edges with water.

To freeze   Wrap each cutlet in polythene film and pack them all in a plastic box. Seal, label, date and freeze.

To finish   Take the cutlets and the béchamel sauce from the freezer. Heat the deep fat to very faintly smoking and drop the cutlets, a few at a time, into the fat. Fry for about 15 minutes, or until the pastry is crisp and golden brown and the cutlet inside cooked through. Drain the cutlets and keep them warm. Turn the béchamel sauce into a saucepan and heat it very gently, stirring constantly. Chop 2 hard-boiled eggs and almost all the cucumber and add to the sauce. Heat it through but do not let it boil. Arrange the chops on a platter, pour a little sauce over them and garnish with the remaining egg yolk, sieved and the egg white finely chopped and with cucumber twists. Pour the rest of the sauce in a sauceboat.

To serve   Serve this dish on a special occasion accompanied with buttered new potatoes and broccoli spears.

Harlequin Ring

The colour of this dessert is quite exquisite and it has the flavour to match.

Serves 8

¾ pint (375ml) frozen double cream
3 eggs, separated
1½oz (37gm) caster sugar
1 miniature Crème de Menthe liqueur

2 teaspoons gelatine
green food colouring (optional)
8oz (200gm) frozen blackcurrants
8oz (200gm) frozen redcurrants

To make   Carefully line a ring mould with polythene film. Take ¼ pint (125ml) of the double cream from the freezer. Put the egg yolks and the caster sugar together in a basin. Add the liqueur and whisk the mixture over hot water until it is thick and frothy. Take off the heat, add a tablespoon of cold water and continue whisking the mixture until it becomes cold again. Meanwhile, dissolve the gelatine in a little warm water, leave to cool, then whisk it into the egg mixture. Add a few drops of green food colouring, if liked. Beat the thawed out cream until it is just stiff, then beat the egg whites. Fold both into the egg and gelatine mixture. Pour the mixture into the lined ring mould.

To freeze   Cover the top of the soufflé with a piece of polythene film and put it in the freezer. When it is frozen, take the soufflé wrapped in the polythene film out of the mould, re-wrap it, if necessary, and put it in a box. Seal, label, date and return to the freezer.

To finish   Take the fruit and remaining cream from the freezer and allow them to thaw out for 2 hours at room temperature. Mix the fruit in a basin and sprinkle with caster sugar to taste. Whip the cream until it is just beginning to thicken. About 1 hour before it is required, take the frozen soufflé from the freezer, unwrap it and put it in a shallow dish. Fill the centre with fruit. Just before serving, pour the half whipped cream over the top.

To serve   Serve this as a light and refreshing end to a meal. Cut the ring in wedges and accompany with a spoonful of fruit and cream.

Index